rororo sprachen
Herausgegeben von Ludwig Moos

Business small talk, die lockere Kommunikation vor, während, neben und nach der Präsentation oder Verhandlung, hat in vielen Ländern einen hohen Stellenwert. Denn die kleinen Gespräche zwischendurch lockern die Atmosphäre und helfen, Vertrauen zu bilden. Vor allem aber sind sie unerlässlich für das *networking*, für das Anbahnen und Ausbauen von Kontakten. Die Deutschen, so geschätzt sie als zuverlässige Geschäftspartner sind, gelten in der Kunst des kleinen Gesprächs nicht gerade als Meister. Doch *small talk* lässt sich lernen. Vor dem Hintergrund einer locker erzählten *business story* zeigen wir Ihnen, wie man Gespräche anbahnt, das Thema wechselt, Schweigen überbrückt, das Eis bricht und wieder zur Sache kommt – kurz, den Partner für sich gewinnt.

Dr. René Bosewitz ist Native Speaker und bereitet in einer deutschen Zweigstelle der London Chamber of Commerce Firmenangehörige auf einschlägige sprachliche Prüfungen vor. Er trainiert zudem seit vielen Jahren Manager aus Banken und Industrie in Business English (mehr Informationen unter www.combenations.de). Bei rororo sprachen hat er *Better Your English* (60802) und *Perfect Your English* (61147) sowie zusammen mit Robert Kleinschroth *Joke Your Way Through English Grammar* (61408) und *Joke by Joke to Conversation* (8795) veröffentlicht.

Robert Kleinschroth unterrichtet Englisch am Gymnasium und an der Universität Heidelberg. Er hat zwanzig Jahre Praxis in der Erwachsenenbildung und leitete fünfzehn Jahre lang die Sprachabteilung eines Großunternehmens. Robert Kleinschroth hat zusammen mit Anne-Laure und Dieter Maupai *Flüssiges Französisch* (61184) verfasst und außerdem *Sprachen lernen* (60842) geschrieben.

Weitere Bände der Reihe Business English sind am Ende des Buches zu finden.

RENÉ BOSEWITZ / ROBERT KLEINSCHROTH

SMALL TALK FOR BIG BUSINESS

BUSINESS CONVERSATION
FÜR BESSERE KONTAKTE

Rowohlt Taschenbuch Verlag

Überarbeitete und erweiterte Neuausgabe Februar 2003
Veröffentlicht im Rowohlt Taschenbuch Verlag GmbH,
Reinbek bei Hamburg, August 1998
Copyright © 1998, 2003 by
Rowohlt Taschenbuch Verlag GmbH,
Reinbek bei Hamburg
Umschlaggestaltung any.way, Wiebke Buckow
Illustration Britta Lembke
Gestaltung Anne Drude
Satz OCR-A und Stone PostScript QuarkXPress 3.32
Druck und Bindung Clausen & Bosse, Leck
Printed in Germany
ISBN 3 499 61446 4

Die Schreibweise entspricht den Regeln
der neuen Rechtschreibung.

Small talk ist keine Nebensache. Gute private und berufliche Kontakte beginnen mit *small talk*. In vielen Ländern steht *small talk* am Anfang und am Ende von Verkaufsgesprächen, Besprechungen oder Verhandlungen. In Spanien und Portugal, in Lateinamerika, Russland und Asien ist die Qualität unserer Waren oft weniger wichtig als der gute Eindruck, den wir als Mensch erwecken. Dort fragen sich unsere Partner zum Beispiel: "Ist das ein Mensch, mit dem wir Geschäfte machen möchten?", "Können wir ihm vertrauen?" und erst danach: "Ist das ein gutes Produkt?" *Small talk* entsteht, so meinen viele, aus einer zufälligen Alltagssituation und endet meist als Eintagsfliege. Tatsächlich jedoch ist *small talk* eine kommunikative Fertigkeit, die man lernen kann, ein Geschick, um mit Dale Carnegie zu sprechen, "to win friends, to influence people and to make people like you" In der Wirtschaft führt *small talk* zu guten Geschäftsbeziehungen, die in gute Verträge münden.

Sie lernen es mit der "Fünf-A-Methode" (im Englischen: Five "E"s)

1. Anbahnung von Kontakten
2. Ausbau mitmenschlicher Beziehungen
3. Austausch von Ideen und nützlichen Informationen
4. Ausforschen von Geschäftsmöglichkeiten für sich und andere
5. Aufbau eines Netzwerks von Beziehungen zum gegenseitigen Vorteil

Natürlich wird der *small-talker* in erster Linie darauf bedacht sein, anregende Gespräche zu genießen und neue Menschen zu entdecken. Aber er behält dabei stets im Hinterkopf, daß es in unserer Dienstleistungs- und Informationsgesellschaft weniger darauf ankommt, was man weiß, als vielmehr darauf, wen man kennt. Das Nebenprodukt sind neue Partnerschaften auf Gegenseitigkeit.

Mit der "Fünf-A-Methode" knüpfen Sie ein Netzwerk von Beziehungen, von denen alle Beteiligten profitieren. Und wenn Sie Glück haben, endet mancher Kontakt in eine dauerhafte Geschäftsbeziehung, vielleicht sogar in Freundschaft.

Begleiten Sie Fritz von Brausewitz in seiner Karriere vom verarmten Adligen zum Großhändler von Schlössern, Titeln und Geistern. Erwerben Sie auf diesem Weg die Strategien und die englischen Redemittel, mit denen Sie mehr aus Ihren persönlichen Kontakten machen. Dies geschieht wie immer mit viel angelsächsischem Witz.

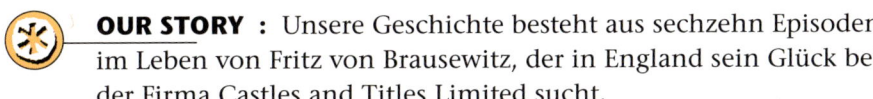

OUR STORY : Unsere Geschichte besteht aus sechzehn Episoden im Leben von Fritz von Brausewitz, der in England sein Glück bei der Firma Castles and Titles Limited sucht.

Small talk SKILLS : In jeder Episode sind ganz bestimmte Fertigkeiten verborgen, die hier übersichtlich vorgestellt und erläutert werden.

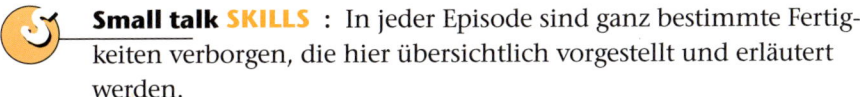

Small talk AWARENESS : In dieser Übung sollen Sie die *small talk skills* in der Story identifizieren, üben oder vertiefen. Die Lösungen finden Sie in den Keys des Anhangs.

Small talk PLUS : Hier geben wir Ihnen zu den behandelten *small talk skills* weitere Redemittel an die Hand, die anschließend geübt werden.

FOCUS : Kurze Texte und Fallstudien führen Sie die Treppe vom *small-talker* zum Netzwerker hinauf. Jede Stufe ist eines der fünf **A** beziehungsweise eines der fünf **E**. Lassen Sie sich überraschen.

WORD AID : Am Ende jedes Kapitels sind die Wörter verzeichnet, die beim Verständnis des Textes helfen.

Small talk AROUND THE WORLD : Im Anhang führen wir Sie in die *Small-talk*-Gewohnheiten von zehn Ländern ein. Die Reise geht von England über Russland, Japan, Korea, China nach den USA.

The small-talker's DICTIONARY ist ein thematisches Glossar für alle möglichen *small talk situations*.

PAIR-WORK on small talk topics bietet Anregungen für das Lernen in Gruppen.

From pub to publisher

There is no business without small talk. You small-talk before, during and after interviews, meetings or presentations, you small-talk at congresses, trade fairs and receptions. Small talk skills are a business "must". When you read our book (we hope with great pleasure) you will notice that there are different types of small talk.

- There's that type of small talk that you use to fill in time. You don't really want to communicate, just to kill time.

- There are also the occasions when you talk about "unimportant" things – the weather, a new car or a new hat.

- Small talk on a higher level is an exchange of information, interesting ideas or opinions. You enjoy a meeting of the minds.

- Then there is small talk which is based on a strategy. This is small talk with a purpose. You communicate with someone who has hidden strategies or wishes.

Experienced businessmen know that often good relations are established, good ideas are born, good contracts are won during informal talks with people who they happen to meet at a conference, on board an aeroplane or at the swimming pool. And it was in this kind of situation that the authors of this series of books first met each other in the Alte Krone pub at Heidelberg. That was more then thirty books ago.

Time for a smile

An exchange of opinions
The other day my boss told me that he'd welcome an exchange of opinions. What he meant by that is that I should come with my opinion and walk away with his.

Guinness and Business

At the pub; Robert Kleinschroth (**K**), head of language training at Carl Freudenberg (CF), Weinheim, René Bosewitz (**B**), Personal Executive Language Consultants P.E.L.C., Annette Sauter (**A**), from P.E.L.C.

K: Well, it's certainly a pleasure to be enjoying a glass of Guinness here with you. By the way, how long have you been in Germany?

B: For about seven years, teaching all over the country.

K: I'm very happy that you were willing to help us with our seminar at CF. We were having a bit of a problem with the business English component of the seminar.

B: It was a pleasure, Robert. It's all part of the service. And CF is an important company. How long have you been involved there?

K: Well, I guess I've been working with them for, let me see, six years.

A: That's quite a long stretch. Don't you feel ready for a change?

K: You can say that again. You know when you're organising or teaching you might try to do your job well. But it's like the eternal law of teaching. If your student is good, then it's because he's intelligent. If your student is bad, well, you're the teacher, so it must be your fault.

A: That's what René has been complaining about for the last three or four years, too.

B: That's right. Actually that was the reason why I decided to start writing books. Do you happen to know my Penguin English Grammar? Well, it's not very profitable, but at least you've got something in your hand. But that got a bit dry and boring, too.

K: I wanted to describe English grammar through jokes but I'm afraid I'd never get a publisher to print it. I've got the jokes. I've been collecting them.

B: Grammar and jokes? Hmm ... then you should rhyme the rules.

A: That's brilliant! Why don't you two work together? What's it called, yes, that's it – synergy. Don't worry about the publisher, René has them eating out of his hand.

B: Oh, you're beginning to sound like a manager, Annettchen. Robert, I think we've got it. Put it there. (*Sound of hands slapping.*)

By the way, that was ten years ago to the day and the beginning of ten years of book writing: a result of small talk – or was it the Guinness?

From small talk to big business

One small talk skill is telling a story when the right moment has come. Business people who try to promote quality, productivity, team spirit and customer service should be aware of the power of story-telling to mobilise people. Communication has more impact when you tell a story to illustrate a point. Follow the example of great leaders from Jesus to Ghandi. They knew about the power of stories. Here is an anecdote that illustrates the title of our book.

A dash of Sir Duncan's

Over one hundred years ago a British nobleman, Sir Duncan Sandys, returned from India where he had been Governor of Bengal. One evening Sir Duncan gave a typical Bengal dinner party for his friends among whom were also two chemists.

In the course of the conversation one of the chemists complimented Sir Duncan on one of the sauces made of several Indian spices which he had particularly enjoyed. "I'll let you have the recipe, if you promise to keep it secret", said Sir Duncan generously.

Eventually the two chemists started to produce the sauce on a small scale. Out of gratitude they sent Sir Duncan as many bottles as he needed for his banquets and that is how the sauce became much talked about in high society.

I'm sure you've tasted their sauce, too. Today it is used throughout the world. The chemists named it after the county in which they lived. Their names? Mr John W. Lee and his partner William Perrins from Worcestershire, the English pronounce it "Wuster". One of many examples of how small talk can result in big business.

WORD AID

aware; be ~ of something	*sich einer Sache bewusst sein*
collect	*sammeln*
complain about	*sich beschweren über*
component	*Teil*
county	*Grafschaft*
course; in the ~ of	*im Verlauf von*
dash	*Spritzer, Schuß*
decide	*beschließen, entscheiden*
describe	*beschreiben*
enjoy	*genießen*
establish a relationship	*eine Beziehung herstellen*
eternal law	*ewiges Gesetz*
exchange	*Austausch; austauschen*
exchange of opinion(s)	*Meinungsaustausch*
fault	*Schuld, Fehler*
fill in time	*Zeit überbrücken, ausfüllen*
generous	*großzügig*
happen to meet	*sich zufällig treffen*
impact	*Wirkung, Effekt*
involve; be involved with	*zu tun haben mit*
mean by	*verstehen unter*
occasion	*Gelegenheit*
opinion	*Meinung*
particularly	*besonders*
pleasure	*Vergnügen*
publisher	*Verleger*
purpose	*Absicht, Zweck*
put it there!	*schlagen Sie ein!*
recipe	*Rezept*
relationships	*Beziehungen*
rule	*Regel*
secret	*geheim; Geheimnis*
skill	*Fertigkeit*
sound like a manager	*wie ein Manager reden*
spice	*Gewürz*
stretch; a long ~	*eine lange Zeit*
the other day	*neulich*
trade fair	*Messe*

Chapter   HOW IT ALL BEGAN

* **OUR STORY:** Fritz von Brausewitz – From soldier to salesman

* **FOCUS:** The nature of small talk
  From small talk to network –
  The five "E"s

* **Small talk AWARENESS:** Small talk international

* **Small talk PLUS:** Avoid foul language and enrich your vocabulary

* **WORD AID:** At the end of each chapter you'll find vocabulary to help you with the texts

Time for a smile

Small talk makes your business partners feel at home, even though you wish they were.

What to say when introduced to a homosexual couple:
"How do *you* do?" and "How do *you* do?"

Fritz von Brausewitz – From soldier to salesman

Once upon a time there was a fairy tale country called Teutonia where everybody could work and earn money and certainly liked to earn money. That was a few years ago. Times change and so did Teutonia. The government fell into an eternal sleep, jobs disappeared, the money dwindled and the jobless inherited the kingdom of Teutonia.

Our hero, Fritz von Brausewitz, had been a well-respected member of the society of Teutonia. He had even studied in Edinburgh for some years. Following a family tradition he served in the Teutonian army, then later as a major he received the golden handshake from the ministry and retired at the age of forty-two.

Alas, the last few years had brought misery to Teutonia (no money to go eating sausage and beer in the lovely beer gardens for which the country is so well-known). He was in real-estate, buying and selling houses and land. However, because of the many rules and regulations involved with houses, architects, taxes and the famous government authorities called "Ämter", Fritz von Brausewitz became less and less successful and more and more frustrated.

Our hero decided to try out foreign parts. "Perhaps I can make a go of it where I'll have more freedom." Of course, nowadays there are no carrier pigeons to transport the news, so von Brausy had to use the Internet. And there he saw the following message in the Times:

We seek a gentleman of character

RESPONSIBILITY:
to negotiate the purchase and resale of properties of the Lords and Ladies of the land.

REQUIREMENTS:
You must have experience in dealing with the cultured classes.

REMUNERATION: linked to success

CONTACT: R. Devenshire, OBE Castles and Titles Incorporated,
Winners Street, York.

FOCUS 1 : The nature of small talk

Before we go on with our story, let's have a look what small talk is all about. In a society where the people are the product and information is the currency it's not so important what you know, as who you know. From good contacts to good contracts it is often just a small-talker's step.

At a cocktail party George Bernard Shaw was asked by his host why he was talking to himself. "I like talking to intelligent people," he replied. At that party there was either no intelligent small talk going on, or the literary genius was unable to join in or enjoy it. Maybe he did not know what small talk is all about.

What small talk is not

▶ Small talk is more than a casual "Hi, how are you today?" as you walk down the hall.
▶ It is more than social niceties to kill time at dinner parties.
▶ It is more than meaningless chit-chat leading nowhere.
▶ It is not a filler to overcome an embarrassing silence.
▶ It is more than talking about the weather.
▶ It is more than story-telling or joke-cracking.
▶ It doesn't mean being clever and witty.
▶ It doesn't require the gift of the gab.

What small talk is all about

In our anecdote Shaw wanted to listen to intelligent people. But small talk has nothing to do with IQ.

▶ It has, however, a lot to do with EQ, the Emotional Quotient.
▶ It is has a lot to do with people skills.
▶ It is a social skill that can be learned.
▶ Small-talkers take interest in other people.
▶ They are good listeners.
▶ They want to make other people feel comfortable.

And last but not least small talk can be a valuable business skill that leads to great contacts and good contracts.

FOCUS 2 : From small talk to network – The Five "E"s

Small talk without a purpose

In this book we distinguish between three levels of small talk. The first is small talk pure, innocent small talk without any thought of how to profit by it professionally. This is small talk without a purpose. If you are a good small-talker you are a "Two-E-Expert" because you

1. enjoy the moment and the company
2. encourage others to participate and engage in satisfying contact with people

Small talk with a purpose

Small talk is not only a social skill, but also a business skill. Business people engage in small talk with a purpose to

3. exchange information and ideas with others
4. explore a new business opportunity

The fourth E means creating contacts through small talk with people you are professionally interested in.

Small talk for networking

It's not important what you know, but who you know. Small- talkers with a vision try to find a place in a network of partners who collect and ex-change useful information over a longer period of time. The effective networker makes the most of his personal contacts. He is the "Five-E-Expert": He wants to

5. establish and expand a network as a bridge to professional success.

More about networking in later chapters.

A **Small talk AWARENESS : Small talk international**

Some nations thrive in the cocktail party atmosphere, others do not. Some may be talking endlessly when they are amongst themselves, however, when they meet foreigners, they are never sure what to talk about. You are German, you travel a lot, you have met people from other countries and we suppose that you have already made some contacts.

Which group of nations do you think is very good (**1**), good (**2**), average (**3**) or weak (**4**) when it comes to small talk with foreigners? Mark them from 1 to 4 and compare with our rating in the key.

Nations	Mark
British, Americans	
Chinese, Russians	
French, Australians, Canadians	
Finns, Swedes, Japanese	
Mexicans, Peruvians, Argentinians	
Germans	

Time for a smile

The following story might help you a little with the rating:
James Peabody, director of a company in the Midlands, welcomed an important customer from Germany. "We're so pleased to have you with us. I do hope you'll enjoy your stay. On Monday night you'll be my guest at the club. You'll meet a lot of interesting people and there's a lot of drinking and ..."
"I'm sorry, sir", interrupted the German. "I don't drink."
"Oh really? Let me see. Tuesday night! You'll like that. We always have a dance. There are lots of pretty girls. You'll really enjoy that."
"No, sir," said the German. "I don't go in for that sort of thing."
"Really? Hmm ... excuse me if I'm being indiscreet.
Are you homosexual?" asked Peabody.
"Certainly not, sir."
"What a pity! In that case you won't enjoy Friday night either."

Small talk PLUS : Avoid foul language!

When small-talking with native speakers of English it might be that you are confronted by unexpected words and phrases. One of these words is "fuck". This word is slang and rude, but can also be used to give more power to what the speaker is saying. Here are some examples:

Phrase:	Real meaning:
Fuck it!	Forget about it. It's not important.
Fuck off!	1. Go away! Clear off!
	2. (with a special intonation) You must be joking!
What the fuck?	It doesn't matter anyway.

These "fuck" words are made to play a grammatical role, too.

As an adjective:
A fucking good film.   A really good film.
It's not my fucking problem.   I'm not involved in it.

As a noun:
What the fuck did you mean?   What did you want to say by that?
I don't give a fuck.   I don't really care about it at all.

Note!
Normally, a well-educated speaker should not be using these words. You, as a foreign learner of English, should not use "fuck" words at all. You will be mis-understood.

17

 **WORD AID** AID

alas	*ach!, leider*
avoid	*vermeiden*
castle	*Schloss*
casual	*lässig, flüchtig*
chit-chat	*Plausch, Schwatz*
contacts	*Beziehungen, Kontakte*
convey ideas	*Ideen vermitteln*
crack jokes	*Witze reißen*
currency	*Zahlungsmittel, Währung*
disappear	*verschwinden*
distinguish	*unterscheiden*
dummy	*Dummkopf*
dwindle	*schwinden, weniger werden*
embarrassing silence	*peinliches Schweigen*
emphasis	*Nachdruck, Betonung*
encourage	*ermutigen*
enjoy	*genießen*
eternal sleep	*Dauerschlaf*
fairy tale	*Märchen*
female	*weiblich*
foreign parts	*fremde Länder*
foul language	*vulgäre Ausdrücke, Sprache*
gift of the gab	*Redegewandtheit*
golden handshake	*goldener Handschlag (Frühpensionierung bei großzügiger Abfindung)*
host	*Gastgeber*
inherit	*erben*
involved; be ~ with	*zu tun haben mit*
jobless	*arbeitslos*
linked to success	*erfolgsbezogen*
mind; give someone a piece of one's mind	*Geist; hier: jemandem seine Meinung sagen*
nicety	*Nettigkeit*

OBE	*Order of the British Empire*
offend	*beleidigen*
opportunity	*günstige Gelegenheit*
property	*Eigentum*
purchase	*kaufen; Kauf*
purpose	*Absicht*
quiet	*Ruhe; ruhig*
rating	*Einstufung*
real-estate	*Immobilienbranche*
remuneration	*Vergütung, Gehalt*
requirements	*Anforderungen*
resale	*wiederverkaufen; Wiederverkauf*
responsibility	*hier: Aufgabenbereich*
sensitive ears	*empfindliche Ohren*
shovel	*Schaufel*
similar to	*ähnlich wie*
skill	*Fertigkeit*
thrive	*hier: aufblühen*
title	*(Adels-)Titel*
valuable	*wertvoll*
vital importance	*große Bedeutung*

AT THE INTERVIEW

- ✳ **OUR STORY: Applying for the Job of castle-seller**
- ⏱ **Small talk SKILLS:** Pay special attention to how to
  - create a friendly atmosphere
  - make people remember your name
  - build a bridge to your partner
  - take a stand (to show your personality)
  - shine but don't be arrogant
- ➕ **Small talk PLUS:** More phrases and tests for small-talkers

Time for a smile

George Bernard Shaw, the famous anti-small-talker,
to Churchill on their first encounter:
"I never forget a face, but in your case I'll make an exception."

Applying for the job of castle-seller

And so it transpired that von Brausy applied for a job in England. And surprise, surprise, he was invited for an interview. It is our task to observe what he says and how he manages everything.

Mr Roger Devenshire, OBE (**R**), Fritz von Brausewitz (**B**),
Mr Andrew Dobson (partner in the company) (**A**)

R: Well, Mr von Brausewitz, it's a great pleasure to have you here with us today. We're very grateful that you could give us some of your valuable time.

B: Not at all. I take every opportunity to visit Britain with its variety of charms whenever I can.[1] By the way, I know my name's a bit complicated for English people to pronounce. Please call me Fritz. I think you have a famous cartoon character called Fritz?[2]

R: Yes, we have. Fritz the Cat. Fritz, allow me to introduce Andrew Dobson, my partner in this little enterprise.

A: How do you do?

B: How do you do? ... Dobson? You're not related to any of the Dobsons near Edinburgh, by any chance? I studied there for two years.[3]

A: Well actually I have a cousin there who has a car showroom. He's also called Andrew.

R: Well, it's a small world, isn't it? Okay, perhaps we might proceed to a few things about yourself ... (*fade out*)
(*fade in*) And so to some of the reasons for your wanting to come over to England. You mentioned in your CV that political and social matters were important for your leaving Teutonia. Surely there were other factors.

B: Well, of course there were several factors. One of them was the way our government is destroying enterprise and motivation in general, which has annoyed me a little.

A: Don't you think that it's the same in every industrial country, Fritz? It's not a special feature of Teutonia.

[1] Small talk skills, die Gegenstand des Kapitels sind, werden durch Hochzahlen gekennzeichnet.

B: Oh, I see it a little differently. There are a whole range of activities which our government has undertaken without the slightest interest in the well-being of the nation.[4] For example... (*fade out*)

R: (*one hour later; fade in*) Well, we've just about come to the end of our interview together, Fritz. It's been very interesting from our side to hear your opinions on business and politics on the continent and to get to know something about real-estate in Teutonia. It seems to be a totally different market.

B: Yes, I think so, but with the right tools you can fight your way through and in my present company's case we are holding our own. I hope I've contributed my bit to that success.[5]

R: I'm sure you have. Well, for our part I think we've got what we wanted to know. Fritz, I'm sure we'll be hearing from each other in the next few weeks. Well gentlemen, if you'll excuse me.

 **Small talk SKILLS**

Good small-talkers don't follow rules. They find the right words naturally without being aware of it. We listen to them and observe how they do it. Creating the right atmosphere, finding the right words at the right moment is what we call skills.

1. Create a friendly atmosphere

Good small-talkers enjoy the conversation and want their partners to enjoy it, too. Brausy used a compliment. Direct personal compliments are dangerous. First, they are often insincere; second, they can be misunderstood as flattery. Brausy complimented Roger indirectly: *I take every opportunity to visit Britain with its variety of charms whenever I can*. It's safer to praise your partner's country, secretary or car. (see **Small talk plus 1**)

2. Make your name memorable

Brausy dropped a "brain anchor" into Roger Devenshire's memory. He created a pleasant association between his name and a very popular English cartoon. *"Please call me Fritz. I think you have a famous cartoon character called Fritz?"* This association will help Roger to remember Fritz.

3. Build a bridge, meet them on common ground

After having been introduced the next step is to find something to small-talk about. Brausy was lucky enough to remember the Dobson family. *You're not related to any of the Dobsons near Edinburgh, by any chance?* You'll always find something you have in common with others: the service at the restaurant, the food, a hobby, the same car etc. (see **Small talk plus 2**)

4. Take a stand to show your personality

Small talk means engaging in a satisfying exchange of ideas. Good small-talkers do not only talk about a topic, but about their relationship to that topic: they take a stand, they show that they have formed an opinion about it. Your opinions are part of your personality. Let's see how Brausy did it: *I see it a little differently. There are a whole range of activities which our government has undertaken without the slightest interest in the well-being of the nation.* Be honest! Nobody likes 'yes-men'. The most self-assured people in business are also the most interesting. In our language box you will find useful phrases to agree and disagree with your partner. (see **Small talk plus 4**)

5. Shine but don't boast

In today's information and service economy, people are the product and information is the currency. Successful people are good at self-marketing. They act as it says in the Bible: "Don't hide your light under a bushel." Eighty percent of success is letting the right people know what your strengths are. A good small-talker knows when the moment has come to do it in a modest and tactful way.
I think so, but with the right tools you can fight your way through and in my present company's case we are holding our own. I hope I've contributed my bit to that success. (see **Small talk plus 5**)

23

Small talk PLUS 1 : Create a friendly atmosphere

I appreciate that you are sacrificing your valuable time.	*Ich weiß es zu schätzen, dass Sie uns Ihre kostbare Zeit opfern.*
Let's forget the formalities.	*Lassen wir die Förmlichkeiten beiseite.*
Make yourself comfortable.	*Machen Sie es sich bequem.*
Do sit down.	*Aber setzen Sie sich doch.*
Can I offer you a drink?	*Kann ich Ihnen etwas zu trinken anbieten?*
Help yourself to some more.	*Gießen Sie sich noch etwas ein.*
This has been a most pleasant conversation.	*Dies war ein sehr angenehmes Gespräch.*

TASK 1: Spot the mistake

Here are more phrases to create a friendly atmosphere with. But this time we have built one mistake into each sentence. Can you spot it?

Haben Sie eine angenehme Reise gehabt?	Did you have a good voyage?
Es ist schön, Sie wieder bei uns zu haben.	It's beautiful to see you here again.
Ich möchte Ihnen zu aller erst danken, dass Sie sich die Mühe gemacht haben, zu ...	I want to begin by thanking you for having made yourself the trouble to ...

You will find more phrases in the *Small-talkers dictionary* where we have listed more than 300 phrases and gambits for small-talkers.

Time for a smile

Host:	May I offer you something to drink?
Guest:	A glass of wine would be fine.
Host:	Certainly. Red or white?
Guest:	It doesn't matter. I'm colour-blind.

Small talk PLUS 2 : Build bridges, find common ground

It's easy to start a conversation. Wherever you meet someone you have something in common to talk about: the weather, the restaurant, the compartment on a train, the same hotel etc. These are bridges between yourself and strangers.

Nasty weather, isn't it?	*Scheußliches Wetter, nicht wahr?*
What a slow train it is!	*Das ist aber ein langsamer Zug!*
How do you find the service in this hotel?	*Wie finden Sie den Service in diesem Hotel?*
It's rather cold/hot/crowded in here, don't you think?	*Es ist ziemlich kalt/heiß/voll hier, finden Sie nicht auch?*
Nice place. Do you come here often?	*Es ist nett hier. Kommen Sie oft hierher?*
I'm from Germany.	*Ich bin aus Deutschland.*
Where are you from?	*Wo kommen Sie her?*
By the way, my name is Meier.	*Übrigens, ich heiße Meier.*
Are you here on business?	*Sind Sie geschäftlich hier?*

Small talk PLUS 3 : Bridges for conferences and trade fairs

Trade-fairs and congresses are ideal meeting points to engage in small talk with the purpose of exploring new business opportunities. Let's suppose you're at an international congress in New York. What do you have in common with the other people? Well, you are all strangers so don't be shy! Everybody would like to meet one person at least. Join a group and try the following bridges:

Excuse me, where is the conference room?	*Entschuldigen Sie, wo ist das Konferenzzimmer?*
Are you here for the first time?	*Sind Sie zum ersten Mal hier?*
Do you happen to know the guest speaker?	*Kennen Sie den Gastredner zufällig?*

What do you expect from the congress?	Was erwarten Sie sich von dem Kongress?
Which hotel are you staying at?	In welchem Hotel sind Sie?
We could have dinner together, if you like.	Wir könnten zusammen zu Abend essen, wenn Sie wollen.

TASK 2: **Guided translation**

1. I beg your pardon, where is the (*Informationsstand*), please?
2. Are you here (*geschäftlich*)?
3. (*Darf ich fragen*) why you are here?
4. (*Wohnen Sie auch im*) the Hilton?
5. (*Was erwarten Sie*) from this congress?
6. Can you (*empfehlen*) me a good restaurant?
7. (*Entschuldigen Sie*), may I (*einen Blick werfen*) at your program?
8. Can you tell me where the press conference (*stattfinden wird*)?

 # Small talk PLUS 4 : Take a stand – say what you mean

Small-talkers are not missionaries who try to convert you to their attitude to life. They are flexible and leave some space for manœuvre. That's why we do not recommend the following opening phrases.

I'm absolutely certain that ...	Ich bin absolut sicher, dass ...
It's my firm belief that ...	Es ist meine feste Überzeugung, ...
It's quite clear that ...	Es ist völlig klar, dass ...
It stands to reason that ...	Gesunder Menschenverstand sagt, dass ...

Tell them what you think, but don't generalise. Use understatement or make your statement personal using opening phrases.

| Well, of course I'm not an expert, but I thought ... | Nun, ich bin natürlich kein Fachmann, aber ich dachte ... |
| I'm not sure, but I for my part would say that ... | Ich bin nicht sicher, ich persönlich würde sagen, dass ... |

| As far as I'm able to judge ... | Soweit ich es beurteilen kann ... |
| I tend to think that ... | Ich neige zu der Ansicht, dass ... |

TASK 3: Spot the mistake

More phrases for expressing your opinion. Can you spot the mistakes?

1. If you would ask me, I would say that we should buy Irish castles.
2. I see it a little different. Irish castles are too small for a golf hotel.
3. How I see it, German castles are more suitable for wine-growers.
4. What me concerns, I think we should only sell titles.

 Small talk PLUS 5 : Shine but don't boast

You know what boasting means? It is the opposite of being modest or clever. You are boasting when you introduce yourself as a landscape technician, a news presenter or a transportation executive and in reality you are only a gardener, newspaper boy, or a van driver. Educated native speakers of English do the exact opposite.

1. They use little words like *a bit of, a little, some, quite, rather, slight, would, might* to soften their statements.
2. They use positive adjectives instead of negative ones, or vice versa: *very good* becomes *not bad at all*. They use antonyms: *not an amateur* instead of *professional*.

Time for a smile

"How do you do?" is a greeting, not a question.
So don't tell people about your indigestion.

John: How do you do?
Hans: General state of health fairly satisfactory. Slight insomnia, blood pressure low, digestion slow.

Don'ts	Do's
I can speak English.	I know some English.
I am a computer specialist.	I have some experience with computers.
I'm a marketing expert.	I'm not exactly an amateur in marketing.
I have a house in Paris.	I have a little house in Paris.
We're the market leader.	Some people might think we're the market leader.
Our cars are first rate.	I think our cars aren't bad at all.
I can solve the problem.	I might be able to solve the problem.
I have a brilliant idea!	Wouldn't it be a good idea to ...?

Time for a smile

How to shine without boasting

It may be your own personal view that two and two make four, but since England is a democratic country others may be of a different opinion. An English professor of mathematics would say to his maid checking the shopping list: "I'm not good at arithmetic, I'm afraid. Please correct me, Jane, if I'm wrong, but I believe that 12 bottles of champagne at £14 each is £168 and not £186."

Adapted from Georges Mikes, How to be an Alien.

WORD AID

anchor	*Anker*
annoy	*(ver)ärgern*
antonyms	*Wörter gegenteiliger Bedeutung*
appointment	*Verabredung, Termin*
appropriate	*angemessen*
attitude to life	*Lebenseinstellung*
boast	*angeben, prahlen*
build bridges	*Brücken bauen*
bushel	*hier: Scheffel*
charm	*Reiz*
common ground	*Gemeinsamkeit*
common; have in ~	*gemeinsam haben*
contribute	*beitragen, beisteuern*
convert someone	*jemand bekehren*
currency	*Währung*
cv (curriculum vitae)	*Lebenslauf*
destroy	*zerstören*
disease	*Krankheit*
drop; ~ anchor	*Anker werfen*
encounter	*Begegnung; begegnen*
encourage	*ermutigen*
enjoy	*genießen*
enterprise	*Unternehmen*
exception	*Ausnahme*
feature	*Eigenschaft, Merkmal*
flattery	*Schmeichelei*
for our part	*was uns angeht*
grateful	*dankbar*
hold one's own	*sich durchsetzen*
indigestion	*Verdauungsstörung*
insincere	*unaufrichtig*
insomnia	*Schlaflosigkeit*
instead of	*anstatt*
join a group	*sich einer Gruppe anschließen*
margin	*Spielraum; Rand; Spanne*

modest	bescheiden
observe	beachten; beobachten
opinion	Meinung
opportunity	Gelegenheit; Möglichkeit
permit	erlauben; Genehmigung
popular	beliebt
pressure	Druck
proceed to	schreiten zu, übergehen zu
purpose	Zweck, Absicht
real-estate	Immobilien
related to	verwandt mit
relationship	Beziehung
satisfactory	befriedigend, zufriedenstellend
service economy	Dienstleistungsindustrie
shine	sein Licht leuchten lassen
showroom	Ausstellungssaal
slight	gering, leicht,
soften a statement	abschwächen
space for manœuvre	(Verhandlungs-)Spielraum
state of health	Gesundheitszustand
suggest	vorschlagen
suitable	geeignet, passend
suppose	annehmen, vermuten
take a stand	Standpunkt beziehen
task	Aufgabe
tool	Werkzeug, Mittel
topic	Thema
trade-fair	Handelsmesse
transpire	hier: durchsickern
understatement	Untertreibung
undertake	unternehmen
valuable	wertvoll
van	Lieferwagen
variety	Vielfalt, Abwechslung
vice versa	umgekehrt
view	Ansicht, Meinung
well-being	Wohlergehen

MIND YOUR MANNERS

Chapter 4

OUR STORY: A first lesson in social rhetoric

Small talk SKILLS: Six golden rules on how to make a good impression

Small talk AWARENESS: Introduction right and wrong
Test your business etiquette

FOCUS: Introducing oneself and others
How to remember names

Time for a smile

How to introduce yourself effectively
The ageing actor was trying to chat up a gorgeous young girl.
"Don't you recognise me?" he asked. She shook her head.
"But I'm quite well-known in the movies," he went on.
"Oh!" she said and her eyes lit up. "Where do you usually sit?"

✳ A first lesson in social rhetoric

Fritz von Brausewitz (**B**) began to feel after two weeks in England that good as his English was, it lacked that nuance, that way to manage as one will, in other words a lack of rhetoric and small talk. He joined a seminar called *Rhetoric For You* with Paul Carpenter (**P**), the small talk consultant.

P: Now, Fritz, first tell me, have you already attended a seminar like this?

B: Well, I've done quite a few rhetoric seminars ... presentations, negotiation, telephoning and all that.

P: Hmm, I see. Business skills are one thing but social skills are another.

B: I know that creating good relationships is necessary for success in business.

P: In successful negotiating the two things are inseparable. Actually, small talk is a non-business skill, but as important for success in business as negotiating or presenting.

B: But I've always thought that it's a talent that some people have and others don't.

P: I make a living from those who don't have it. Let's start with the basics, with situations that are foreseeable, like introducing, welcoming or greeting, and then we can enter the minefield of the more unpredictable situations. And so the first matter is how to greet people and introduce yourself. How would you do that?

B: Perhaps "How do you do?"

P: Much too formal in a small talk situation. You can start with "Hi, I'm Fritz von Brausewitz." And your partner might say "Hi, Joe Kowalski." Next time you meet him you address him by his name. Have you got a good memory for names?

B: I've a memory like a sieve, but I'm good with faces.

P: Well, repetition does the trick. Give yourself more time to memorise his name: "Kowalski? How do you spell that, with a "y" or an "i" at the end?" Or "Kowalski? That's a Polish name, isn't it? Do you speak any Polish?" You can try to make a personal bridge to the person with: "Joe, that's my brother's name, too. What a small world!"

B: My goodness! It's all more complicated than I thought. Are there other tricks to learn?

P: Don't worry! You probably do half the things naturally anyway. There are some things to keep in mind when introducing other people. For example, when introducing two peers to each other you can say either name first. Mention first name and last name. And help them to find some common ground: "Oscar Osborne, this is Bryan Hemmung. Like yourself he has a keen interest in the modern theatre." This extra information helps them to memorise each other's names and they have something to talk about.

B: I have to be more careful with bosses. I've been having trouble with them.

P: Just remember! Always mention the name of the superior first. And it's the same if you're introducing customers. Treat them as if they were the superior.

B: And what about shaking hands? In my country when we are introduced we should stand up and offer our hand for the famous handshake.

P: It's the same here. And if you can, when you greet somebody for the first time, use a "tag line" as we call it: It's a bit more information about yourself. Depending on the situation: "Hi, I'm Fritz Brausewitz from Castles and Titles in York. I'm in the business of buying castles."

B: Okay. I get the picture. What else can I do to get closer to other people, to customers, for instance?

P: Of course there are many techniques once you've got through the basic introduction. Oh, I almost forgot. Here's a poster with six golden rules for your pinboard since you've got a memory like a sieve.

 **Small talk SKILLS**

Six golden rules on how to make a good impression

The first encounter is the most important moment in a relationship. You never get a second chance to make a good impression. That's why you should keep our IMPACT-Formula in mind:

Integrity means being honest and truthful with business partners.
Manners means never being selfish, rude or undisciplined.
Personality: communicate your own values and opinions.
Appearance: wear suitable clothes, stand and sit in a good posture.
Consideration: see yourself from the other person's standpoint.
Tact: think before you speak; avoid religion, sex and politics.

(A) Small talk AWARENESS

TASK 1: Introduction right and wrong

The first five sentences. Here's a little test. You'll find the solutions in the key.

1. Let's suppose you are Fritz von Brausewitz. You are introduced to Paul Dobson. What will he say?

   A. How do you do, Mr Brausewitz?
   B. How are you, Mr Brausewitz?
   C. Good day, Mr Brausewitz.
   D. Pleased to meet you, Fritz.

2. Now Fritz, what is your reaction?

   A. Fine, thank you.
   B. And how are you?
   C. How do you do?
   D. Pleased to meet you, Mr Dobson.

3. The following day you meet Mr Dobson again? How do you greet him?

   A. How do you do?
   B. How are you, Mr Dobson?
   C. How are you?
   D. Hi, Paul.

4. And how will Mr Dobson react to your greeting (see 3.)?

   A. I feel a bit sick.
   B. Fine, thank you.
   C. How are you?
   D. Thank you, fine.

5. You get on very well with Paul Dobson and you invite him to your home. He suggests using first names. What will he say?

   A. By the way, call me Paul.
   B. Call me Paul.
   C. I'm Paul.
   D. My first name's Paul.

FOCUS 1 : Introducing oneself and others

Introducing yourself

Americans and young Brits are the most uncomplicated nations. Very quickly they are on first name terms. They walk up to you, stick out their hand and say:

James: Hi, I'm James, James Kelly.
You: Pleased to meet you. My name's Fred, Fred Allen.

Tom: I'm Anthony Neil. Everybody calls me Tony.
You: Nice to meet you, Tony. I'm Fred, Fred Allen.

Can you see the difference between the two introductions? In the second you repeated Tony's name. First, it's more personal; second, you have heard the name and used it; this will help you to remember it.

Introducing peers

It doesn't matter who is introduced first.
Try to repeat the name and add some additional information that both people are interested in. This could serve as a bridge to enjoyable small talk.

You: Mike, I'd like you to meet René Bosewitz. He is my co-author.
        René is the official representative of the London Chamber of
        Commerce in our area.
        René, this is Mike Disney. I know Mike from hospital where he
        had his bits and pieces operated on.
René: Pleased to meet you, Mike. You must tell me more about that
        operation.

Introducing a higher ranking person to a lower ranking

Although in today's business world matters of rank are no longer as important as they used to be, you should nevertheless observe some rules, especially when the persons are conservative or belong to the older generation.

Who is considered to be higher ranking?

superiors   hosts and hostesses   guests

customers   older persons   women

What to do:

▶ Say the name of the higher ranking person first.

▶ Introduce the newcomer.

▶ Add some information to establish common ground.

▶ Mention titles

Mr Bosewitz, I'd like you to meet Ratty ..., sorry, Tony Rattigan. He is un-employed at the moment, but he seems to be a good jogger.

Tony this is Dr René Bosewitz, author of the best-selling novel "How to phone effectively". He is a regular jogger like yourself.

TASK 2: Test your business etiquette

1. Is it true what they say about the English?
   A. The English shake hands only in formal encounters.
   B. Businessmen don't shake hands.
   C. They shake hands. It all starts with a handshake.

2. Brausy has an appointment with Lord Pembroke, who is waiting for him in his office. What do you think is most likely to happen?
   A. Lord Pembroke will stretch out his hand first.
   B. Brausy takes the initiative.
   C. Shaking of hands is not appropriate in this situation.
   D. They stretch out their hands simultaneously.

3. And if you shake hands how long should you normally hold the other person's hand?
   A. For one second.
   B. For two or three seconds.
   C. For five seconds.

4. A typical question: 'Do you get a lot of rain in Kiel?'
   A. Yes, I'm afraid of it.
   B. Yes, I'm afraid we do.
   C. I'm afraid, yes.

FOCUS 2 : How to remember names

One of the best ways of building a relationship with somebody is to remember their name the next time you meet, and where you last met. People like to be remembered. Remembering someone's name shows that you care about them. However, we tend to forget names after a couple of days, weeks or months. Here is some advice on what to do about it:

How to remember names

▶ As you shake hands with someone, repeat their name aloud: "Nice to meet you, James."
▶ Good small-talkers use each other's names as often as possible, in order not to forget them.
▶ As you say it look at their face and store it in your memory.
▶ See their face with their name written on it.
▶ Hear your voice saying the name.
▶ Feel your lips producing the sound.
▶ With some names you can ask them to spell it: Is it Bert with an 'e' or a 'u' as in Burt Lancaster?
▶ If you exchange cards note down where and when you met them.

When you meet them the following year they will be flattered to be addressed by name.

What to do if you have forgotten a name

You are at your usual holiday resort, somebody walks up to you and says: "Hi, Bob. Don't you remember me? We met in X last year."
And you can't recall his name. What do you do?

▶ Wait and hope that you will remember in the course of the conversation?
▶ Confess that you can't recall his name. Don't be ashamed. It happens to everybody. Admit that you have a bad memory for names.

WORD AID

additional information	*Zusatzinformation*
admit	*zugeben, eingestehen*
ageing	*alternd*
appointment	*Termin, Verabredung*
appropriate	*angemessen, schicklich*
attend a seminar	*ein Seminar besuchen*
chat up a girl	*ein Mädchen anmachen*
depend on	*abhängen von*
establish common ground	*Gemeinsamkeit herstellen*
flatter	*schmeicheln*
formal encounter	*förmliche Begegnung*
gorgeous; a ~ girl	*ein hübsches Mädchen*
gossip	*Klatsch*
holiday resort	*Ferienort*
impact	*Wirkung, Effekt*
invariably	*immer, unweigerlich*
keen; have a ~ interest in	*ein starkes Interesse an ... haben*
lack something	*etwas nicht haben, an etwas fehlen*
make a living	*seinen Unterhalt verdienen*
memorise something	*sich etwas merken*
mind your manners	*achten Sie auf Ihre Manieren*
movies	*Filme, Kinos*
peer	*Gleichgestellte(r)*
recall a name	*sich an einen Namen erinnern*
recognise someone	*jemanden erkennen*
remind someone of	*jemanden erinnern an*
sieve	*Sieb*
superior	*Vorgesetzter*
unpredictable	*unvorhersehbar*

- **OUR STORY:** A big fish on Brausy's hook
- **Small talk SKILLS:** Discover something about others
- **Small talk AWARENESS:** Recognising small talk skills
- **Small talk PLUS:** Pay special attention as to how to
  - apologise
  - show sympathy
  - make compliments
- **FOCUS:** The First **E:** Enjoy the moment and the company
  What to talk about
- **Small talk PLUS:** Drop anchors in their memories

Time for a smile

TV interviewer: Well, just one last question, Mr Bush, and we can conclude this interview. Have you heard the latest political jokes?

President Bush: Heard them? I appointed them all!

⊛ A big fish on Brausy's hook

Von Brausewitz had a good interview and was able to convince the directors of the English company. Two weeks later he received a letter saying he was appointed sales consultant specialising in the area of castles and estates for the aristocracy. Four weeks later he is on his way back to London to begin his new career.

> On board a plane. Brausy (**B**), by accident sitting next to
> Lady Emily Gilmore (**E**), stewardess (**S**)

(Sound of aeroplane engines)

B: Oh my god! What pressure in my ears.

S: Hello sir, are you okay? You look a bit pale.

B: I feel a bit pale. It's all this turbulence. I'm not used to flying.

S: Don't worry, sir, it's all perfectly normal.

B: Normal. (*To Lady Emily*) My father used to say "If God had intended man to fly he would have given us wings."[1] I hope I haven't disturbed you with my neuroses.[2]

E: Oh, it's no problem at all.

B: You seem very composed. I suppose you travel regularly, perhaps on business or simply for pleasure?[3]

E: Both actually, I travel with my father, Lord Gilmore of Firth.

B: (*to himself: "My goodness, I'm meeting the aristocracy already; got to meet this girl again"*). Firth in Scotland? Why, I've visited it many times.[4] A wonderful part of the country and so peaceful.[5]

E: Yes, we think so too. But daddy's not too happy at the moment.

B: Oh, nothing serious, I trust.

E: Well, we've got financial problems. We may have to sell our ancestral home.

B: (*to himself: Great! What an opportunity!*). Oh, I'm so sorry to hear that.[6] I know what it is like. My father had to sell our little castle. The costs were too high.[4] Perhaps everything will work out for you in the end. I myself am interested in architecture and buildings. It's one of my hobbies.[7]

E: Well, with all the travelling I don't have much time for hobbies.

B: No hobbies, at all?

E: I do try to keep fit. I do a bit of horse-riding. We play the occasional game of squash.

B: Do you indeed? So do I, though in Teutonia where I come from, we're certainly not as skilled at squash as you English.[8] I think you invented it.

E: As far as I know it was invented by prisoners in Australia.

B: Indeed. I didn't know that. But then if you think about it most of the games we play were invented by the British – tennis, golf, football, squash, rugby, boxing etc. An ingenious race.[5] I myself have very little time because of my work.

E: What line are you in, Mr eh?

B: Von Brausewitz, "Brause" is a fizzy drink and "witz" means joke.[9] I'm a dealer in noble homes.[10]

E: A dealer in mobile homes? Do you mean camping buses?

B: Noble homes, rather immobile ones. Actually I buy and sell castles in Teutonia and in England.

E: Oh, that sounds profitable.

B: The money is of no importance. As I said, architecture is my hobby. My company concentrates on old properties that should be preserved for posterity (*Change in engine sound*) My goodness! What was that?

E: We're coming in to land. Time passes quickly when you're talking, doesn't it?

B: Yes, it does. We'll soon be in London. Do you have a hotel you like to stay at?

E: Yes, the Trafalgar in the West End. We've used it for years.

B: What a coincidence! I've reserved a room there, too. I really hope we'll meet again.[11] Thank God we're down. May I help you with your luggage?

 **Small talk SKILLS**

As a good small-talker Brausy is interested in discovering something about another human being. He is excited about what is around the next corner, he small talks for the same reason as he reads books. However, he is also ready to give. Giving and getting makes small talk satisfying for everybody. Don't follow the example of the famous author who, after talking to a young lady for half an hour about himself, finally said: "Let's talk about you for a change, my dear. How did you like my latest book?"

Let's see in Task 1 how Brausy did it on the plane.

A Small talk AWARENESS

TASK 1: Recognising small talk skills

There are numbers in the dialogue. They refer to small talk skills.
Put the right number next to the skill. The first has been done for you.

1	Use a one-line joke that suits the occasion as an ice breaker.
	Be interested in your partner's situation. Show sympathy.
	Be considerate. An apology is a good small talk starter.
	Use your hobbies to build bridges to your partner's interests.
	Watch your partners. Are they in the mood to small talk? Talk about what you're thinking at the moment
	Make them a gift. Find something to compliment them on.
	Find common ground.
	Make your name memorable.
	Be modest. Give them the feeling that they are superior.
	Make your job interesting. Create yourself a tag line.
	Prepare the next encounter.

Small talk PLUS 1 : Apologising

I hope I haven't disturbed you with my neuroses, said Brausy. An excuse is one
way to start a conversation. It provokes a reaction: *Oh, it's no problem at all.*
Some small-talkers will step on your foot, push you, take your coat, read your
newspaper only to have something to apologise about and to establish the
first contact.

How to apologise	How to react
Oh! Was that your foot? I'm ever so sorry.	Never mind.
Oh! This is your glass. I can't tell you how awfully sorry I am.	Never mind! That's all right.
I'm afraid I mistook your suitcase for mine. I just don't know what to say. I owe you an apology.	Please don't worry. These things happen.
I do apologise. I thought it was my coat. We seem to have the same taste.	Don't worry about it. We all make mistakes, don't we?

Making excuses to start a conversation

"Excuse me ..." and "I beg your pardon ...". "I'm sorry, but ..." and "Please forgive me ..." are very often used as an introduction when you

- want to get information
- start a conversation
- criticise someone

If you go on with "but ..." an excuse can become a reproach or criticism.

> Excuse me, is this seat taken?
> I beg your pardon, I think we've met before.
> I'm sorry to trouble you, but this table has been reserved.

 # Small talk PLUS 2 : Showing sympathy

If you are not interested in people, they won't be interested in you. Having sympathy for others is one way of showing that you are interested in them. This is how Brausy did it: *Oh, I'm so sorry to hear that. I know what it is like. My father had to sell our little castle. The costs were too high.*

How to show one's sympathy

I'm sorry to hear that.	*Es tut mir Leid, das zu hören.*
I know what it's like.	*Ich weiß, wie das ist.*
I can imagine how you must feel.	*Ich kann mir vorstellen, wie Sie sich fühlen.*
It's a great loss to us all.	*Es ist für uns alle ein großer Verlust.*
I don't know what to say.	*Ich weiß gar nicht, was ich dazu sagen soll.*
Please accept my sympathy.	*Darf ich Ihnen meine Anteilnahme aussprechen?*

Time for a smile

> Tom: My wife says she will leave me if I don't throw out my computer.
> Fred: Oh, I'm sorry to hear that.
> Tom: So am I. I'll miss her.

TASK 2: Patchwork – apologies, excuses and criticism

afraid		apologise		apology
	excuse me		sorry to	
pardon		forgive me		sorry

Put the patches into the following sentences

1. .... for saying so, but that's the way we've always done it.
2. ...., but that's his job, not mine.
3. ...., darling, not here, somebody might see us.
4. I'm .... have to say this, ...
5. I owe you a bit of an .... I've smoked your last Havana.
6. I beg your ...., but this is my coat.
7. I .... for being late, sir. Has anything happened?
8. I'm .... we all make mistakes, don't we?

 Small talk PLUS 3: Making compliments

Brausy complimented Lady Emily on the beautiful countryside and on the achievements of her people in the fields of sports. Indirect compliments are never embarrassing, while personal compliments ("*You have the most marvellous eyes I've ever seen*") are often understood as primitive flattery. Flattery is telling your partner exactly what he thinks about himself. Praise and compliments, however, should come from the heart. It gives people a feeling of being appreciated, being important.

Making compliments

I think your hat is really great.	*Ich finde Ihren Hut sehr hübsch.*
Your suggestion is brilliant.	*Dein Vorschlag ist genial.*
This dress suits you down to the ground.	*Dieses Kleid steht Ihnen einfach toll.*
The wine's out of this world.	*Der Wein ist nicht von dieser Welt.*
Your stamp collection is second to none.	*Ihre Briefmarkensammlung ist unvergleichlich/einzigartig.*
You certainly know what's what.	*Sie kennen sich aber gut aus.*

TASK 3: Guided translation

1. I hadn't (*erwartet*) such a good interview.
2. I (*habe viel gehört über*) your clever handling of complaints.
3. Your design for the new car (*ist wirklich gut*).
4. (*Was für einen schönen*) garden you have!
5. I'd like to (*beglückwünschen*) you on your latest book.

Time for a smile

Anne: I've heard a lot about you as a small-talker.
Ron: Oh, it's not worth talking about.
Anne: Yes, that's exactly what I've heard.

Witty reactions to personal compliments

The experienced small-talker knows how to react to compliments and flattery: Here are a few witty reactions that won't make the other person feel uncomfortable.

Thank you. You're most kind.
I can live for two months on a good compliment.
I've been complimented many times, and that always embarrasses me. I always feel they haven't said enough.
I graciously accept all compliments. One can't argue with the truth.
Some people say "thank you" after receiving a compliment. I simply nod in agreement.
Thank you for the compliment. I've been collecting compliments all my life. Yours is the third.

Time for a smile

The boss leaned over to his secretary who was busily painting her fingernails and said: Mrs Sauter, I'd like to compliment you on your work, but when are you going to do any?

FOCUS 1 : The First E: Enjoy the moment

You remember the Six "E"s? Let's have a closer look at the first E. Enjoying small talk does not depend on the subject of the conversation. It has more to do with your attitude.

Do's

▶ Relax, listen and join in the conversation.

▶ Try to discover common ground.

▶ Play the game and return the ball. It is a game without winners or losers. No one is your opponent; everybody is your partner.

▶ Enjoy meeting people you are not likely to run into in your business or social life.

Don'ts

▶ Don't wait until someone invites you. Say hello, join them.

▶ Don't try to make points. Small talk is not a debate.

▶ Don't try to convert people to your way of thinking even if you are convinced that it would be for their own good.

▶ Don't try to be clever. You are not in a competition for the "Wit of the Week".

 FOCUS 2 : What to talk about

Small-talkers enjoy a good conversation because they like to discover new people. It is fun trying to find out what is going on inside other people. Are they like me? Are they different? Enjoy discovering their background, experiences, and dreams by listening and talking to them. This is the stuff novels and dramas are made of. "All the world is a stage" says Shakespeare – it's less dramatic than in dramas, but it's a real stage on which you can play an active role. Small-talkers enjoy that. If you do not know what to talk about, here are a few suggestions. You start with anything you have in common with everybody else.

▶ the restaurant: What's your favourite dish?
▶ the atmosphere: I hope you're enjoying yourself.
▶ the place: Are you here for the first time?
▶ the host: How long have you known our host?
▶ people present: Who else do you know at the party?

These are common topics because they are not controversial. The problem is saying something different or personal. See our suggestions in the glossary. You can then talk about what comes spontaneously to mind.

I'm from Berlin. Where do you come from?
I was sent here by my boss. Why are you here?
I drive a Rover. I saw you arrive in the same car. Are you happy with it?
Did you realise we're wearing the same watch? How long have you had it?

Be prepared to have more to say

▶ Read the newspaper every day.
▶ Watch TV.
▶ See good films.
▶ Go to exhibitions, shows and galleries.

The weather

In England this is an everlasting, even thrilling topic, and you must be good at discussing the weather. A conversation like this is typical.

> Nasty day, isn't it?
> I don't like it at all, do you?
> Fancy such a day in July.
> I remember exactly the same July day in 1936.
> Yes, I remember it too.
> Or was it in 1949?
> Yes, now that you mention it, I think it was.

England is a democratic country. They have different weather forecasts for taxi drivers, tourists and farmers:
Weather forecast for farmers: Tomorrow it will be cold, cloudy and foggy. Long periods of rain will be interrupted by short periods of showers.
Weather forecast for tourists: Tomorrow it will be fair and warm with many hours of sunshine.

Small talk PLUS : Drop anchors in their memories

The usual introduction: *I'm Fritz von Brausewitz, Castles and Titles Incorporated* very often dries up when your partner replies: *I'm James Kelly. Pleased to meet you.* And in our hectic world the names will be soon forgotten. There are better ways of making yourself memorable.

I met a dynamic businessman in a Robinson Club. When asked what he did, he introduced himself: "Dietrich Lutz. Erfolgscoach. My aim is your success." – "What do you mean?" was the reaction of a bystander and Lutz had the chance of presenting his firm of consultants and explaining their unique selling proposition. They will remember Dietrich Lutz because he aroused their curiosity and provoked a question. He anchored his name and profession in his partners' memories, instead of simply saying: "I run a firm of consultants." Shakespeare used one of these anchors in Julius Caesar (I,1). Asked what his trade was a shoemaker replied with a clever pun: "I'm a mender of bad soles." (sole: Schuhsohle and soul: Seele). A priest could have used the same line.

Here are some examples to fire your imagination

Hairdresser:	I'm a designer of good looks.
Doctor:	I try to make you live forever.
Language trainer:	I make you speak with a second tongue.
Teacher:	I train the brains of your kids.

TASK 4: Guess who I am

Make yourself memorable, create your own anchors. They should be like riddles to make your listeners think and provide them with the question "What do you mean?" This can be the beginning of some nice small talk. Now here's a little riddle for you to train your brain.

1 I'm the greatest debtor in Germany.
2 I work for you.
3 I work in the field.
4 My aim is your success.
5 I cook the books.
6 I'm the polisher of the staff.

A Consultant
B Personnel manager
C Accountant
D Civil Servant
E Minister of Finance
F Salesman

WORD AID

accidentally	*zufällig*
accountant	*Buchhalter*
achievement	*Leistung*
ancestral; our ~ home	*das Haus unserer Vorfahren*
anchor	*Anker*
apology	*Entschuldigung*
appoint someone	*jemanden ernennen*
appreciate	*schätzen, mögen*
arouse curiosity	*Neugier erwecken*
attitude	*Einstellung, Haltung*
bystander	*Anwesende(r)*
coincidence; what a ~!	*Was für ein Zufall!*
competition	*Wettbewerb*
composed; be ~	*ruhig, gelassen sein*
considerate	*rücksichtsvoll*
convert	*bekehren, missionieren*
convince	*überzeugen*
cook the books	*die Bücher frisieren*
depend on	*abhängen von*
disturb	*stören, belästigen*
embarrassing	*peinlich, unangenehm*
encounter	*Begegnung*
estate	*Anwesen*
excited	*aufgeregt, erregt*
fizzy drink	*prickelndes Getränk*
flattery	*Schmeichelei*
gift	*Geschenk*
hook	*Haken*
host	*Gastgeber*
ingenious; an ~ race	*ein erfinderisches / geniales Volk*
intend	*beabsichtigen*
memorable	*denkwürdig, einprägsam*
mobile home	*Campingwagen*
mood	*Stimmung*
nod	*nicken*

nosy parker	Neugieriger
occasional	gelegentlich
opponent	Gegner
owe	schulden
praise	Lob
preserve for posterity	für die Nachwelt bewahren
pressure	Druck
property	Besitz, Eigentum
provoke	hervorrufen, auslösen
pun	Wortspiel
recognise	erkennen
reproach	Vorwurf
skill	Fertigkeit
skilled	geübt, geschickt
stage	Bühne
suit the occasion	der Gelegenheit angemessen sein
superior	überlegen
sympathy	Anteilnahme, Mitgefühl
tag line	Zitat, Pointe, Markenzeichen
though	obwohl
thrilling	spannend
topic	Thema
unique selling proposition (USP)	einzigartiges Verkaufsargument
used to; he ~ ~ say	er pflegte zu sagen
wing	Flügel, Tragfläche
wit	Mutterwitz; geistreicher Mensch

Time for a smile

Mind your manners: What you should not say to a Scot
I'm your Conservative candidate.
Got any Irish whisky?
Jimmy, where are your trousers?
What do you like about the English?
You would be nothing without your North-Sea oil.

BUILDING BRIDGES

Chapter 6

OUR STORY: Table talk

Small talk SKILLS: Building bridges
Using fade-ins
Interviewing without interrogating
Don't be a wallflower
Springboards
Give before you take
Know when to talk about business

Small talk AWARENESS: Recognising small talk sins

Small talk PLUS: More phrases for small-talkers

FOCUS: The first two "**E**"s

Time for a smile

Eric: I come from a very old military family.
        One of my ancestors fell at Waterloo.*

Ernie: Really?

Eric: It's a fact. Someone pushed him from platform nine.

---

* Waterloo is a train station in London named after the battle of Waterloo

⊛ Table talk

Von Brausewitz (**B**) was, of course, deceiving Lady Emily (**E**) when he told her he was staying at the same hotel as she was. He quickly phoned his own hotel, The Black Duck, cancelled his originally booked room and checked in at the Trafalgar. He waited in the bar until he observed the object of his attention enter the dining-room.

B: How marvellous to meet you here by chance. If you aren't expecting anybody, do you mind if I join you?[1]

E: Not at all. Please do. I hope you've recovered from the flight. It was a bit bumpy.[2]

B: You can say that again. But now that we're on firm ground allow me to suggest a good drop of what your Scotland is so famous for?

E: Isn't it a bit early for alcohol?

B: You mustn't think I'm an alcoholic. I can sometimes go for hours without touching a drop. May I get you anything else, a glass of wine perhaps?

E: Well, I for my part am not used to drinking alcohol, except for an occasional glass of wine for dinner and it's not dinner time yet.

B: Dinner! I would be pleased if you would honour me with your company. As Tennyson says: "You'll have no scandal while you dine, but honest talk and wholesome wine." (*fade out*)

E: (*In the dining room; fade in*) ... so we lived most of our lives in Scotland.

B: I suppose you had a very peaceful life there.[3]

E: Oh, life was pretty busy. I had to run the administration of the castle for my father.

B: But you were saying you had to stop that.[3]

E: Yes. I had always wanted to study so I enrolled at Edinburgh University.

B: Really? Another of those amazing coincidences. I also studied there fifteen years ago. I did a one-year course in applied linguistics for a diploma. What was your subject?[4]

E: I studied translation, Russian and German.

B: Aha! So perhaps we should speak German?

E: Oh no, I'm terribly out of practice. I never had the chance to work in that field. After I finished the course my father began to get into financial problems.

B: Talking of Edinburgh that reminds me of some wonderful things I did at that time.[5] I used to go with some of my fellow students to the islands on the west coast, you know, the Outer Hebrides.

E: I know them well, We had a small house on Uist. It's beautiful.

B: And then there were the walks in the Grampions. And after a day's walking ...

E: You went into a small local pub and had a couple of pints.

B: Exactly. Those were the days! By the way, is it true what I heard on BBC? Scotland is going to become independent?[6]

E: Well, since you ask, I think it's about time we took some responsibility for our own lives up there. But I shouldn't be boring you with our little problems.

B: Boring? Not at all. I certainly won't be able to sort out your political problems, however, financial problems and castles are my speciality.[7] I'd feel honoured, if I could be of any help. But let's not talk business now.[8] It's been such a delightful evening and ... (*fade out*)

Small talk SKILLS

1. **Build bridges:** It is done by association of thought. You use a bridge when you want to move away from one topic to another that is connected with the first. Brausy did this in his conversation with Lady Emily. (see **Small talk plus 2**)

2. **Use small talk fade-ins:** Resume the conversation where you broke it off and you are on common ground again.

3. **Interview without interrogating:** Small talk is soft talk. Interrogating is tough talk. Leave it to the journalists. Brausy did not use questions at all. He just encouraged Emily to go into more detail, to tell more about the topics or the problems she had introduced herself (*I suppose you had a very peaceful life there. But you were saying you had to stop that*). (see **Small talk plus 1**)

4. **Don't be a wallflower:** Join the people you have met before. Good mixers become good small-talkers. Don't be a wallflower, like Ronald:
   Hostess: Would you like a lemon with your tea?
   Ronald: No, I prefer to be alone.

5. **Springboards:** What to do when a topic is exhausted, when you realise that you have touched your partner's sore spot? Then it is time to use the so called "springboard technique". You jump to a completely new subject. Often a silence of four or five seconds is enough to signal that a topic is finished. Your conversation partner will be happy to change the subject. However, there are also linguistic springboards if you feel that silence might be embarrassing. (see **Small talk plus 3**)

6. **Exchange memories:** Talking about childhood, school or university seem to open people up. These are the times when values were fomed, important decisions were made and the first steps in a career were taken. You will notice that their voices change, that they wake up and relax. Listen and encourage your partners and you will get to know them better than by reading their curriculum vitae. (see **Small talk plus 1**: Making them talk)

7. **Give before you take:** Don't ask a personal question without having given the same information about yourself first. Example:
I'm from Berlin. Where do you come from?
My boss wanted me to attend the congress. Why are you here?

8. **Know when to talk about business:** Wine is wine and business is business. Don't explore business opportunities, it might spoil a pleasant evening.

A) Small talk AWARENESS

TASK 1:	**Recognising small talk skills**

During their dinner Emily and Brausy were using some small talk skills. We have numbered them in the dialogue. Can you put the number from the conversation next to the skill? The first has been done for you.

Don't be a wallflower	1
Build bridges	
Exchange memories	
Give before you take	
Use fade-ins	
Use the springboard technique	
Know when to talk about business	
Interview without interrogating	

Small talk PLUS 1 : More phrases for small-talkers

Our second **E**: encourage others to participate in the conversation.
A skilful small-talker does it

- by showing his interest,
- by attentive listening and
- by encouraging his partner.

He fills the pauses with comments of polite astonishment like:

It's amazing.	*Das ist erstaunlich.*
Incredible! Unbelievable!	*Unglaublich!*
That beats everything!	*Das ist einmalig/unerhört!*
Marvellous!	*Wunderbar!*
How interesting!	*Wie interessant!*
Good Lord!	*Großer Gott!*
Good heavens!	*Du meine Güte!*

Astonished questions are not considered as interruptions. They tend to provoke typical reactions:

Really?	It's a fact!
No, really?	It's just as I'm telling you.
Are you sure?	Absolutely!
Are you serious?	I'm dead serious.
Can you believe it?	There's no doubt about it.

Here are a few examples which needn't be taken too seriously.

Time for a smile

Ron: A funny thing happened to my mother in Glasgow.
Bob: Really? I thought you were born in Nottingham.

Eric: I used to be a tough fighter when I was younger. I could lick a man with one hand.
Ernie: No, really?
Eric: It's just as I'm telling you. Unfortunately, I could never find a man with one hand who wanted to fight.
From Eric Morecombe and Ernie Wise

Here are typical phrases to encourage a storyteller. Can you translate them into English? The first one has been done for you.

1	*Aha! Ich verstehe.*	Hmm, I see.
2	*Erzählen Sie mir mehr davon.*	.... me ....
3	*Kaum zu glauben!*	You ....n't .... it!
4	*Ist das wirklich Ihr Ernst?*	Do you .... that?
5	*Was Sie nicht sagen!*	You don't ....!
6	*Das ist höchst interessant.*	That's .... interesting.
7	*Hätte ich nie geglaubt.*	I'd ....

 # Small talk PLUS 2 : Building bridges

Brausy built a bridge from Emily's financial problems to his job as real estate agent: I certainly won't be able to sort out your political problems, however, financial problems and castles are my speciality.

TASK 3: | **Complete the bridges**

Use the correct form of these verbs: *remember, have, remind, talk, hear*

That .... me of a story I .... the other day.
When you mentioned Tom, I .... how I first met him.
I .... a similar experience a couple of years ago. It was in ....
.... about holidays, what are your plans for this year?

 # Small talk PLUS 3 : Springboards

If you feel your partner is losing interest in a subject, bridges and springboards help you to start a new one.

By the way, is it true what I heard on the BBC ...?
You know, I just read an article about ...
What I have always wanted to ask you ....
You might be interested in knowing that ...
I thought of you when I heard ...

Small talk PLUS 4 : Polite noises

TASK 4: Patchwork

	honour		could		
may I		shall			put
	recovered		mind		
should		hope			want

1. If you aren't expecting anybody, do you .... if I join you?
2. I hope you've .... from the flight. It was a bit bumpy.
3. .... get you anything else, a glass of wine perhaps?
4. I would be pleased if you would .... me with your company.
5. But I ....n't be boring you with our little problems.
6. I didn't really .... to waste your time with that now.
7. I .... you're settling in at your new job.
8. I didn't want to cause any trouble. Please let me .... it right now.
9. It's really a bit chilly here. .... I close the window?
10. Perhaps we .... play a game of chess some time.

Table talk anecdote

Suppose you are dining with somebody who is shy and who doesn't return the ball to your court. Then it is up to you to do most of the talking if you want to avoid long periods of embarrassing silence. For these emergencies the experienced small-talker always has a few anecdotes up his sleeve. Here is one.

The architect of the German Empire, Prince Otto von Bismarck, was known to be a stickler on formality. An American woman was seated next to him at dinner one day. She addressed her opening remarks correctly with the title "Your Highness". By the time the second course was served this had become "Mr Chancellor". A course later and she was calling him "My dear Mr Bismark." As the waiters came with the dessert, Bismarck smiled and said, "My first name is Otto."

FOCUS : The first two "E"s

Encouraging is the opposite of interrupting. This is an excerpt from Dale Carnegie, *How to win friends and influence people*. It is a good illustration of the first two "E"s:

▶ How to enjoy small talk
▶ How to encourage your partner

I was recently invited to a bridge party. Personally, I don't play bridge and there was a blonde there who didn't play bridge either. She had discovered that I had travelled a great deal. So she said: "Oh, Mr. Carnegie, I do want you to tell me about all the wonderful places you have visited and the sights you have seen." As we sat down on the sofa, she remarked that she and her husband had recently returned from a trip to Africa. "Africa!" I exclaimed. "How interesting! I always wanted to see Africa, but I never got there except for a twenty-four-hour stay once in Algiers. Tell me, did you visit the big-game country? Yes? How fortunate! I envy you! Do tell me about Africa."

That was good for forty-five minutes. She never again asked me where I had been or what I had seen. She didn't want to hear me talk about my travels. All she wanted was an interested listener, so she could expand her ego and tell about where she had been.

Was she unusual? No. Many people are like that. For example, I recently met a distinguished botanist at a dinner party given by J. W. Greenberg, the New York book publisher. I had never talked to a botanist before, and I found him fascinating. I literally sat on the edge of my chair and listened while he spoke of hashish and Luther Burbank and indoor gardens and told me astonishing facts about the humble potato. I have a small indoor garden of my own, and he was good enough to tell me how to solve some of my problems.

Midnight came. I said good night to everyone and departed. The botanist then turned to our host and paid me several flattering compliments. I was "most stimulating." I was this and I was that; and he ended up by saying I was a "most interesting conversationalist."

An interesting conversationalist? I? Why, I had said hardly anything at all. I couldn't have said anything if I had wanted to without changing the subject, for I don't know any more about botany than I know about the anatomy of a penguin. But I had done this: I had listened intently. I had listened because I was interested.

WORD AID

applied linguistics	*angewandte Sprachwissenschaft*
attend a congress	*einen Kongress besuchen*
attentive listening	*aufmerksames Zuhören*
awareness	*Bewusstsein, Bewusstheit*
bet	*Wette*
big-game	*Großwild*
bore someone	*jemanden langweilen*
botanist	*Botaniker*
bumpy	*unruhig (Flug)*
cancel	*absagen, stornieren*
coincidence	*Zufall*
course	*hier: Gang (eines Menüs)*
curriculum vitae	*Lebenslauf*
dead serious	*todernst*
deceive	*täuschen*
depart	*aufbrechen*
embarrassing	*peinlich*
enrol	*sich einschreiben, immatrikulieren*
expand one's ego	*sein eigenes Ego ausbreiten*
fade-in	*Einblende*
genuinely interested	*wirklich, echt interessiert*
honour someone	*jemandem die Ehre machen*
independent	*unabhängig*
intently	*aufmerksam*
interrogate	*verhören, ausfragen*
join someone	*hier: sich zu jemandem setzen*
lick/beat a man	*jemanden verprügeln*
marvellous	*wunderbar*
nickname	*einen Spitznamen geben*
observe	*beobachten*
occasional	*gelegentlich*
participate in the conversation	*am Gespräch teilnehmen*
pint	*hier: ein Bier*
practice; out of ~	*außer Übung*

prefer	*vorziehen*
recently	*kürzlich*
recover	*sich erholen*
resume the conversation	*das Gespräch wieder aufnehmen*
sight	*Sehenswürdigkeit*
since	*da; seit*
skilful	*geschickt*
sleeve; have something up one's ~	*etwas in der Hinterhand haben*
sore spot	*wunder Punkt*
sort out problems	*Probleme lösen*
springboard	*Sprungbrett*
stickler on formality	*jemand, der es mit Formalitäten sehr genau nimmt; Pedant*
subject	*Fach; Thema*
taciturn	*schweigsam*
topic	*Gesprächsthema*
tough fighter	*harter, zäher Kämpfer*
value	*Wert*
wholesome	*gesund, zuträglich*

Time for a smile

Table talk anecdote
Calvin Coolidge, the taciturn thirtieth President of the United States, was nicknamed Silent Cal.
"I've made a bet, Mr President," said a young woman next to him, "that I can get more than two words out of you."
"You lose," replied her host.

HOW NOT TO BE A WALLFLOWER

Chapter 7

* **OUR STORY:** Getting to know one's colleagues
* **Small talk SKILLS:**   Introducing oneself professionally
                              Integrating a newcomer
                              Reviving a conversation
                              Small talk with a purpose
* **Small talk AWARENESS:** Recognising the small talk skills
* **Small talk PLUS:**   What to say after you have said "Hi"
* **FOCUS:**   How to get integrated
                              Small talk with a purpose

Time for a smile

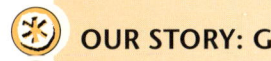

How to switch on girls
"You can't be real. May I pinch you to see if I'm dreaming or not? By the way my name is Meier. I'm here on a business trip."

By the way my name is ... Oh forget it, I'm glad you don't recognise me. I'd rather have you like me for myself.

Getting to know one's colleagues

At the office party. Brausy (**B**); John, Marketing Manager (**J**); Hilary, his wife (**H**); Tim, the accountant (**T**); Amy, wife of Tim (**A**); Richard (**R**) and David (**D**), two fellows from the legal department.

Brausy enters the main office where twenty or thirty people including wives of employees are gathered together. He feels nervous, hangs around by the door. He notices there are in fact several small groups in the room. Remembering a technique he had read in his bible of behaviour "Small Talk For Big Business" he has no problem to open a circle, join the group and get what he wants.

B: Hi, I'm Fritz, the new man.

J: Hi, my name's John, I'm in marketing and this is Hilary, my better half.

B: (*he nods*). Nice to meet you, John.

T: And I'm Tim from accounts. Actually, we were just discussing the future of the company. Perhaps a fresh view like yours could give us a new perspective.[1]

B: (*smiling*) I'll do my best, but don't forget I'm new here. And I must say, although I've travelled a lot in Britain, this is without doubt one of the most charming cities I've been in.[2] I hope I'll be able to have my base here.[3]

A: So you've not managed to find a place yet then?

B: Not yet, unfortunately. You see, I'm not quite sure which part of York might be suitable.

A: Listen, that's no problem. I'll call Hilary over and we'll give you a "wives' guide to living in York". Hey, Hilary, have you got a minute? (*fade out*).

J: (*fade in*) ... so basically I'm fed up with the whole bunch of 'em, left, middle and right.

R: Hear! Hear! A complete waste of our energy and money. (*An hour later. They have been discussing politics and have worn the subject out. The conversation drags on and stops. There is no more energy in the conversation. Fritz tries a new angle on the same topic.*)

B: That's all true but look at it from another point of view.[4] In some countries they only have military regimes. They waste their time killing each other. At least our fighting is done in terms of the economy.

D: Fritz has a point there. Perhaps we should all keep that in mind.

B: Salmon![5]

J: Beg your pardon, Fritz? What did you say?

B: I said salmon. I was just thinking. York is near Scotland and you have excellent salmon in Scotland.

D: Is fishing one of your many talents then, Fritz?

B: It's more a passion than a talent.

D: A passion you have in common with John. He spends most of his weekends on his boat. You should talk to him. He's always on the lookout for someone who'll help him kill and grill our poor finned fellow creatures. John, could you come over here for a moment?

Small talk SKILLS

1. Introducing oneself professionally

Observe how the colleagues introduced themselves. They did not only say their names "Hi, I'm Fritz". They added an identifier that explained who they are and what they do or why they were there. "I'm the new man", "I'm Tim from accountants" etc. It not only helps your partner to remember you. It can become food for small talk. More about identifiers in **Small talk plus 1**.

2. Integrating a newcomer

If newcomers join your group give them a helping hand. After having introduced everybody invite them to participate in your conversation by briefly telling them what you were talking about.

3. Reviving a conversation

What to do when a topic is worn out, when the conversation drags on and stops? Well, you could build a bridge (That reminds me of ...) or use the springboard technique. In our dialogue Brausy tried to look at the subject from a different angle. Did you notice how he did it?

4. Small talk with a purpose

Small talk can be an effective tool to get what you cannot get in another way. It is perfectly all right to see people as walking encyclopaedias and personalised Yellow Pages. In the Yellow Pages you find all the electricians and plumbers in town. During small talk over the garden fence you will find out the most reliable or least expensive ones. Brausy went into the party room with two objectives in mind. We'll quiz you on that in our awareness test.

A) Small talk AWARENESS

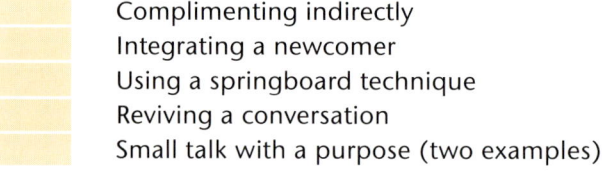

TASK 1: Recognising the small talk skills

We have numbered some small talk skills in the dialogue. Can you put the right number from the conversation next to the skill?

- Complimenting indirectly
- Integrating a newcomer
- Using a springboard technique
- Reviving a conversation
- Small talk with a purpose (two examples)

Small talk PLUS : What to say after you have said "Hi"

The name of your company would be just another name. Here are three suggestions and each serves a different purpose, however, you can also combine them.

1. Make your name memorable by adding an identifier that gives more information about yourself.

2. It's not true that the best conversation opener is the bottle opener. Referring to the situation you are in at that moment can have the same effect. Say what you feel.

3. A clever introduction is the first step towards getting useful information (see also: **Small talk with a purpose**).

    On the next page you will find some examples.

1. Use identifiers: Tell them …

What you do	I'm in marketing. I buy and sell old property.
Where you work	We have an office near the station.
Where you are from	I'm from Berlin.
Who you work for	I'm the personal assistant to the director.

These identifiers usually answer your partner's unspoken questions: *Who are you? Why are you here?* Small-talkers might use your job, your office, your home town or your boss as bridges or springboards to start a conversation.

2. Use the situation

What situation are you in?	I'm the new man.
	I seem to be the only stranger here.
	This is my first conference. I'm kind of lost.
Talk about your feelings.	I'm Paul Smith. I'm so glad I could get to this meeting.
How are the persons related to each other?	You all seem to know each other.
	How does it come that you all know each other?

Mentioning the situation you are in or your feelings are signals that you want to be integrated. There will always be someone who understands these signals.

3. Tell them what you want

Say why are you here	I'm here to learn more about marketing on the Internet.
Who do you want to meet?	I'm hoping to meet people who have experience with castle-buying.
What do you want to get?	I'm here because … why are you here?

Why should people want to help you? Well, three people out of five enjoy being of help to a newcomer. It gives them a feeling of superiority. Older persons like to help the younger generation.

FOCUS 1 : How to get integrated

FIRST STEP : How to enter a room full of strangers

Shy people have stage fright entering a room and joining a group. They go into the restroom and spend some time checking whether their tie or make-up is correct. Therefore they are rarely among the first to enter the room and so they often enter a room which is already full of strangers. They hesitate to walk to the middle of the room. They are afraid that everybody might stop talking and look at them. They try to be invisible and look straight ahead so as not to meet another person's eyes.

Experienced small-talkers recognise shy persons, walk up to them, say "hallo" and introduce them to their group. Timid people make good contacts. They might not be very entertaining, but they will be grateful and won't forget your assistance when you ask them a favour.

If you feel awkward entering a room full of strangers, remember that most of those present don't know each other either. Nobody expects your arrival, nobody will pay attention to a newcomer – unless you are a celebrity or the guest of honour. And if you are you shouldn't have any problems anyway.

Don'ts

▶ Don't be worried about your make-up or your clothes, put on a pleasant smile, that is all the make-up you need.

▶ Don't stand close to the doorway.

▶ Don't play the wallflower. Don't stand with your back to the wall.

▶ Don't stand with your arms crossed over your chest.

▶ Don't look around demonstratively, as if you are looking for a friend. It keeps others from approaching you.

Do's

▶ Relax. Stroll to the middle of the room.

▶ Say "Hi" to people as you walk past.

▶ Take a drink if offered. You needn't drink it but with a glass of champagne you at least know what to do with your hand.

▶ Join a group of strangers.

SECOND STEP : How to join a group

Let's suppose you are on your own in a bar, at a meeting or at a congress. People are standing around in groups. They naturally form a circle. Don't hesitate to open it by touching someone's arm gently but firmly. Almost always the circle will open to allow you come in. You won't be the only stranger. Everybody will think that you know at least one member of the group.

- ▶ Don't interrupt a speaker by introducing yourself.
- ▶ Seek eye contact with the speakers.
- ▶ Use body language: smile and nod in agreement with what people say.
- ▶ Make polite noises: *Ah! Of course! How interesting!*
- ▶ Listen until you find a chance to introduce yourself or to contribute to the conversation.

THIRD STEP : How to beat a retreat

You are looking for your friend, Fred. You discover him standing in a group talking. Don't break into the group when you can see that a private conversation is going on. If you realise too late, make a polite retreat.

What to say

Oh, I'm sorry I didn't want to intrude on your conversation.
This seems to be a private conversation. I'll catch you later.
OK, Fred, may I talk to you later?
Oh, you're busy. I'll come back later.
Oh, you're having a tête à tête. We'll see each other later.
Sorry, I see you want to be alone. See you later.

Recognising an in-group

You can recognise an in-group by watching them talk:

- ▶ Are people touching each other?
- ▶ Do their faces express emotion?
- ▶ Are their voices lower or higher than normal?

FOURTH STEP : Forming your own group

If you don't feel like joining a group you can form a group of your own.

▶ Look for a person who is standing around alone.
▶ Introduce yourself.
▶ Start a conversation.

What to say

This is an interesting evening, isn't it?
Excuse me, may I join you for a beer?
You don't seem to know anybody here?
We seem to be the only strangers here.
Are you here for the first time? – So am I.
I didn't expect it to be so good tonight, did you?
Normally I'm not into parties, but this one is really good.

TASK 2: Guided translation

1. Hilary, have you (*einen Moment Zeit*)?
2. John, could you (*mal kurz rüberkommen*)?
3. You all (*scheinen sich zu kennen*).
4. Is fishing (*eines Ihrer vielen Talente*), Fritz?
5. That's all true but look at it (*von einer anderen Seite*).
6. I'm here (*um mehr über ... zu lernen*) marketing on the Internet.
7. (*Ich hoffe, Leute zu treffen*) who have experience with computers.

Time for a smile

Sir Alec returns to his London club, fresh from his holiday in France. "Did you have a good time?" his friends ask him. "Yes, excellent", he says. "Did you have any problems with the language?" "No," says Sir Alec, "I didn't, but the French did."

FOCUS 2 : Small talk with a purpose

You remember the first two "E"s of small talk? They are the basis from which to go to the third E.

Enjoy the small talk
Encourage your partner
Exchange useful information and ideas with others

THE THIRD E : Exchanging useful information

The experienced small-talker shows his interest by attentive listening. He encourages his partner with phrases that show sympathy and involvement. This can lead to a useful exchange of ideas and information. In a small talk situation everybody is off-duty, but they are in a market where they swap information and ideas. This does not mean that you are exploiting your partner as long as you do not seek advice for which he or she normally sends people a bill. You can expect this kind of free advice only from friends. So don't ask a doctor for a free prescription for your heartburn nor a lawyer about your troubles with the tax people. On the other hand, small talk situations are a stock exchange of free information not to be had elsewhere. Don't be shy! You are only asking for information, not for money, a job, work or confidential information.

When you have moved to another city like Brausy did, there are a lot of things money can't buy. Brausy entered the room with two aims in mind:

1. He wanted to find a flat in York. He was clever enough to mention it during the introductions:
   B: *I hope I'll be able to have my base here.*
   A: *So you've not managed to find a place yet then?*

2. He was looking for someone to go fishing with. He used the springboard technique:
   B: *Salmon!*
   J: *Beg your pardon, Fritz? What did you say?*
   B: *I said salmon. I was just thinking. York is near Scotland and you have excellent salmon in Scotland.*

Your list of small talk objectives

The experienced small-talker enters a small talk situation with a "shopping list". This might be the list for someone who has moved to a new city:

▶ the right school for children
▶ a student to help your children with their homework
▶ a reliable babysitter
▶ the best tennis club in town
▶ where to buy cheap office furniture
▶ a veterinarian surgeon who makes house calls

Nothing is more flattering than honest attention and interest. If your neighbour at the coffee table or in a conference has any information to offer that you have been looking for, you add a grain of flattery:

You can certainly recommend some good books on this.	*Sie können mir sicher ein paar interessante Bücher empfehlen.*
May I phone you up about the authors and the titles?	*Darf ich Sie wegen der Autoren und Titel anrufen?*

Make a list of what you have to offer

Remember, small talk is not a one-way street. Always think about what you could offer in return. Be prepared. Make up a list of what you have to give. Here is our list, which is by no means complete.

▶ a good language school in Britain
▶ a book or an article someone could need
▶ the right publisher for someone's book
▶ our experience on how to deal with certain publishers
▶ how best to learn a foreign language
▶ which fitness centre to avoid in Heidelberg
▶ where to get a job as a language teacher
▶ how to deal with local authorities if you are a foreigner
▶ tested learning-software for adults and kids etc.

WORD AID

accountant	*Buchhalter*
accounts	*Buchhaltung(sabteilung)*
advice	*Rat*
aim	*Ziel*
angle	*Blickpunkt*
approach someone	*jemanden ansprechen, sich nähern*
attentive listening	*aufmerksames Zuhören*
avoid	*(ver)meiden*
awareness test	*Bewußtseinstest*
awkward; feel ~	*verlegen sein*
base	*Stützpunkt*
bunch; the whole ~	*die ganze Bande*
celebrity	*Berühmtheit*
chest	*Brust*
confidential information	*vertrauliche Informationen*
contribute	*beisteuern, beitragen*
desperately	*verzweifelt*
doubt	*Zweifel*
drag on	*sich hinziehen*
fed up with	*die Nase voll haben von*
finned; our ~ fellow creatures	*unsere beflossten Mitgeschöpfe*
flattering	*schmeichelhaft*
gather	*versammeln*
grain	*Korn; Körnchen*
guide	*Führer; führen*
hang around	*herumstehen*
heartburn	*Sodbrennen*
hesitate	*zögern*
identifier	*Erkennungszeichen*
include	*einschließen, inbegriffen sein*
intrude on	*sich aufdrängen, einmischen*
invisible	*unsichtbar*
join someone	*sich jemandem anschließen*
least expensive	*am billigsten*

legal department	*Rechtsabteilung*
lost; be ~	*verloren sein; sich nicht auskennen*
observe	*beachten; beobachten*
one-way street	*Einbahnstraße*
participate	*teilnehmen*
passion	*Leidenschaft*
pinch	*kneifen, zwicken*
plumber	*Klempner*
prescription	*Rezept; Verschreibung*
purpose	*Zweck; Absicht*
recognise	*(wieder)erkennen*
refer to	*verweisen auf; Bezug nehmen auf*
restroom	*Toilette*
revive	*wiederbeleben*
salmon	*Lachs*
seek advice	*Rat suchen*
seek eye contact	*Augenkontakt suchen*
shyness	*Schüchternheit*
springboard	*Sprungbrett*
stage fright	*Lampenfieber*
stock exchange	*Börse*
stroll	*schlendern*
superiority	*Überlegenheit*
suppose; let's ~	*nehmen wir einmal an*
swap information	*Informationen austauschen*
switch on girls	*Mädchen anmachen*
tie	*Krawatte*
tool	*Werkzeug; Mittel*
veterinarian surgeon	*Tierarzt*
wallflower	*Mauerblümchen*
waste	*Verschwendung*
worn out	*abgenutzt; erschöpft*
Yellow Pages	*die Gelben Seiten*

INSENSITIVE SMALL TALK

Chapter 8

(*) **OUR STORY: Trying too hard at the customer's**

(S) **Small talk SKILLS:** A closer look at
- how to interrupt
- how to be tactful
- how to small-talk with a purpose

(A) **Small talk AWARENESS:** Five small talk sins

(+) **Small talk PLUS:** Interrupting a speaker

(F) **FOCUS:** Small talk is dialogue
Stopping the boring small-talker

Time for a smile

A group of tourists were visiting a castle in Scotland. The lord, a handsome young man wearing a kilt, was boring his audience to death with endless explanations about Gothic architecture and Scottish traditions. Finally a pretty girl who couldn't stand this any longer interrupted his monologue.

"By the way, I've just remembered what I wanted to ask. What is worn*under your kilt?"

With a fine smile the Scotsman replied: "Nothing is worn, my dear. Everything is in perfect working condition."

* wear, wore, worn: tragen; abnutzen

Trying too hard at the customer's

Brausy sets off for Castle Newbury, a small estate with an 18th century mansion, a small wood, a river and a lake. The owner, Sir Anthony Reed, is an elderly impoverished aristocrat who is no longer able to pay for the repairs of the castle. And so the bailiff pays Sir Anthony regular visits.

Sir Anthony Reed (**A**), Fritz von Brausewitz (**B**)

B: Well, thank you for that excellent lunch, Sir Anthony. Now let's turn to our business. I was really interested in your stories about golfing in this area.

A: Yes, but sadly those days are numbered, I think we …

B: (*interrupting*) It's no problem. You'll always find time for a round or two.[1] How long did it take you to get down to a handicap of four?

A: You don't learn it overnight. It required more than a decade. Perhaps I should have spent more time working on my accounts and less on the golf. Then I wouldn't be in this situation. I hope you …

B: The problem with the British aristocracy is that you don't know how to run an estate. You shouldn't see the black side.[1] By the way, you must have been a professional in your time. Did you win all these trophies over there yourself? Of course you did, didn't you?[2] Why don't we go on the course tomorrow. You could show me a few tricks.[3]

A: I'm not sure. Some fresh air would certainly do me good after all this trouble with the bailiffs.

B: By the way, could you advise me which golf club I could join for my business connections and all that? Aren't you president of the local golf club? Yes, I saw it on your letterhead.[2]

A: Well, I don't know if …

B: (*interrupting*) Well, you scratch my back, and I'll scratch yours. What I'm needing is a course within 35 miles of here. Can't lose too much time travelling[3]. Time is money, as you yourself know.

A: Only too well. Perhaps I can think of something after we have discussed the selling price of the estate and so on … (*fade out*)
(*fade in*) And so we were hoping to get a higher price because of the wood, lake and river.

B: Well, it's worth considering. By the way what sort of fishing does your river offer?

A: Just some peaceful trout fishing. It's ...

B: (*interrupting*) That won't help very much. Salmon's the thing nowadays. Have you done any salmon fishing yourself?[4]

A: Yes, I did a little in Scotland and Ireland when I was younger.

B: Yes, it reminds me of times a few years back when I was a student in Edinburgh. We would go to the west coast every weekend, rent a boat and fish to our hearts' content. You had to get up at four o'clock in the morning. There were all sorts of different trout. They have different ones in each loch, you know. But as I said, I'm more interested in salmon. My father used to spend his holidays in Norway. Norway is famous for its salmon, you know and ...[5]

A: Yes, I do know. Mr von Brausewitz, if you will excuse me now it's almost midnight and I'm an old man and I'm actually feeling very tired. You know you are our guest at Castle Newbury tonight. James will show you to the library if you want to have a nightcap. Have a good night.

 **Small talk SKILLS**

1. Interrupting a speaker

A good conversation has a natural flow. Let it take its course, don't paddle against the stream or try to change its direction. An abrupt interruption is only admissible if you want to help or offer something. In all other cases use a more polite way of doing it.

On the other hand, interruptions can be the motor of a good conversation. The more lively it is, the more enthusiastic the participants are, the more frequently it will be interrupted. Good small-talkers provoke witty comments, they pause for two seconds to invite a question, they notice and respond to reactions.

Sometimes it is necessary to interrupt a selfish small-talker who dominates the conversation, who wants to have the first, the middle and the last word. (see **Small talk plus**: Interrupting a speaker)

How to be an impossibly bad small-talker

- Interrupt when you lose interest.
- Interrupt subordinates because you have the higher status.
- Interrupt when you cannot contribute.

- Interrupt women; they always confuse small talk with gossip.
- Look repeatedly at your watch while listening.

2. How to be tactful

A sensitive small-talker does not force a subject onto his partners. He abandons a topic when he feels that his partner is not interested. He listens patiently when he feels that his partner wants to talk about personal problems. On the other hand, you should not bother other people with your own worries.

How to be insensitive

- Don't listen when someone is trying to explain something.
- Talk for more than five minutes about yourself.
- Look the other way when someone is going to open his heart to you.
- Ask questions and answer them yourself.
- When someone asks you a question jump to the next topic.
- Tell your stories with all the details.
- Always have the last word.

3. Small talk with a purpose

The experienced small-talker engages in conversations with a "shop-ping-list". Brausy has two things on his list: a lesson with an experienced golfer and easy access to a golf club for business connections. However, he has forgotten two things:

1. Your shopping list should be accompanied by a list of things you have to offer in return. Don't abuse your host by asking favours that you should be asking for in a more formal situation.

2. Never ask for advice for which your partner could send you a bill. Don't ask a doctor for a free prescription, a top tennis player to play tennis with you if you are a mediocre player or a lawyer for advice in legal matters.

4. Small talk with a smile

It wasn't all Brausy's fault. Sir Anthony Reed was in a gloomy mood because of his hopeless financial situation. There's only one thing that is more contagious than cheerfulness, and that is the lack of it. Maybe Sir

Anthony's miserable face is the explanation for Brausy's lack of sensitivity. Nobody wants to to deal with a "misery", so the first **E** (enjoy the moment and the company) was missing during the conversation.

Remember that a smile
- is the shortest distance between two people
- is a little curve that puts everything straight
- makes the other person respond more positively

 A **Small talk AWARENESS**

TASK 1: Are the following statements true (T) or false (F)?

Brausy has come to Newbury with two purposes in mind.
Brausy has been over-interrupting Sir Antony.
Sir Anthony is interested in fishing and golfing.
Sir Anthony thinks that Brausy is a bad small-talker.

TASK 2: Five small talk sins

In the dialogue we have numbered five sins you should avoid. Can you put the right number from the conversation next to the sin? The first has been done for you.

Don't talk too long.	5
Don't force a topic onto your partner.	
Don't be insensitive to your partner's situation.	
Don't ask questions that you answer yourself.	
Don't ask for favours without having something to offer.	
Don't unlock memories that your partner cannot share with you.	

Time for a smile

Advice to after-dinner speakers:
If after ten minutes you don't strike oil, then stop boring.

Small talk PLUS : Interrupting a speaker

How not to interrupt

Hang on.	Moment mal.
Sorry to butt in, but ...	Entschuldigen Sie, wenn ich Ihnen ins Wort falle, aber ...
Sorry to break in, but ...	Tut mir Leid, wenn ich Sie unterbreche, aber ...

TASK 3: Guided translation

A more tactful way of interrupting

1. How fascinating! That (*erinnert mich an*) ...
2. I'd like to (*etwas hinzufügen*) here, if I may.
3. I (*möchte Sie nicht*) to interrupt you, but ...
4. Excuse me, sir, may I (*Ihnen eine Frage stellen*) ?
5. Excuse me, but may I (*spielen*) the devil's advocate (*für einen Augenblick*)?

TASK 4: Patchwork: How to go on after being interrupted

Put the patches where they belong.

go		return		answer
	to what		continue	
took		coming		saying

1. As I was ....
2. If I could just ....
3. To .... to my subject ...
4. .... back to my story ...
5. Going back .... I was saying ...
6. To .... back to what I was saying ...
7. I'll .... your question in a minute.
8. You .... the words right out of my mouth.

FOCUS 1 : Small talk is dialogue

Brausy was not a good small-talker at Castle Newbury. He talked for too long about memories. Here are a few rules about what a dialogue really is.

Monologue	Dialogue
Ask no questions	Ask questions
Answer your own questions	Wait for others to answer
Talk for more than three minutes	Notice and respond to reactions
Fill up silences	Be comfortable with little silences
Ignore newcomers to the group	Involve newcomers

Here is a small talk example from the British TV series Faulty Towers. Basil, the hotel owner, comes with the breakfast for Mr Leeman, one of the guests. He is looking at the newspaper as he goes. He knocks and enters. Inside Mr Leeman is sitting in bed, his eyes open. Basil enters and puts the tray down in front of Mr Leeman.

Small talk with a corpse

Good morning! Breakfast! Here we are. (*Basil picks up a book from the floor and puts it down on the bedside table*) Another car strike. Marvellous, isn't it. (*He goes to the window and draws the curtains*) Taxpayers pay 'em millions each year, they get the money, go on strike. It's called Socialism. I mean if they don't like making cars why don't they get themselves another bloody job designing cathedrals or composing viola concertos? The British Leyland Concerto in four movements, all of 'em slow, with a four-hour tea break in between. I'll tell you why, because they're not interested in anything except lounging about on conveyor belts stuffing themselves with my money. You don't mind if I turn the light off? (*He does so and turns to Mr Leeman as he opens the door*).
Well, enjoy your breakfast... I'm sorry, I didn't catch that ... Oh, not at all, thank you for mentioning it. (*He exits, closing the door, and starts off down the corridor*) Un-be-lievable. Not a single bloody word. You get up at five-thirty so they can lounge around in bed till midday and do you get so much as a word of thanks?

As you might have guessed, Mr Leeman is lying dead in his bed.

FOCUS 2 : Stopping the boring small-talker

What to say

1. Inform them that you have ended your small talk session and would like some quiet.
2. Or simply comment: "Thank you for giving us a piece of your mind. It's a pity you don't have much left."
3. Or you could say: "I hear you are going into hospital next week for a brain operation – the doctors hope to give you one."
4. Or "The last time I saw something that looked like you, I threw it a peanut."

How to use body language

1. Look at your watch repeatedly.
2. Tap the glass of your watch with your finger.
3. Turn your face away.
4. Walk away.

How to stop small-talkers during operas and concerts

1. If others are small-talking behind you, give them dirty looks.
2. If necessary, pelt them with popcorn.
3. If, while giving them dirty looks and / or pelting them with popcorn, you notice they are bigger and younger than you, gather your belongings and move.

Time for a smile

The man in the front row of the opera was making strange noises very loudly during a tender love scene on the stage. "Shut up!" hissed the audience around him, but still the man continued with his "Oooohs" and "Aaaaahs". Eventually the manager was called and he marched down the aisle until he came to the noisy man. "Get up! You are ruining the performance" demanded the manager. "Ooooh! Aaaaah!" shouted the man in reply. "Where are you from?" asked the manager. "F ... fr ..." groaned the man, "from ... the ... balcony."

WORD AID

access	*Zugang*
accompany	*begleiten*
admissible	*zulässig, erlaubt*
advice; seek ~	*Rat suchen*
aisle	*Gang*
avoid	*vermeiden*
back	*Rücken*
bailiff	*Gerichtsvollzieher*
bill	*Rechnung*
body language	*Körpersprache*
bore	*bohren; langweilen*
bother	*belästigen; bekümmern*
brain	*Gehirn*
catch; I didn't ~ that	*Ich habe das nicht verstanden*
connections; business ~	*Geschäftsbeziehungen*
contagious	*ansteckend*
conveyor belt	*Fließband*
course	*hier: Golfplatz*
demand	*verlangen*
enthusiastic	*begeistert*
estate	*Anwesen*
eventually	*schließlich*
favour	*Gefallen*
flow	*Fluss; fließen*
gather one's belongings	*seine Sachen packen*
gloomy mood	*trübsinnige Stimmung*
gossip	*Klatsch, Tratsch*
groan	*stöhnen*
hearts' content	*Herzenslust*
impoverished	*verarmt*
insensitive	*gefühllos, taktlos*
interrupt	*unterbrechen*
involve newcomers	*Neuankömmlinge mit einbeziehen*
legal matters	*rechtliche Angelegenheiten*

letterhead	*Briefkopf*
lounge	*hier: faulenzen*
mediocre	*mittelmäßig*
misery	*hier: Häufchen Elend*
nightcap	*Gutenachtdrink*
peanut	*Erdnuss*
pelt	*bewerfen*
performance	*Aufführung; Leistung*
piece; give a ~ of one's mind	*seine Meinung sagen*
pity; it's a ~	*es ist jammerschade*
provoke	*herausfordern, provozieren*
require	*erfordern*
respond	*reagieren, beantworten*
sadly	*leider, traurigerweise*
scratch	*kratzen*
selfish	*egoistisch*
sensitive	*einfühlsam*
session	*Sitzung*
sin	*Sünde*
stage	*Bühne*
stand something	*etwas aushalten*
straight	*gerade*
strike oil	*auf Öl treffen*
subordinate	*Untergebener*
tender	*zart*
trophy	*Trophäe*
witty	*geistreich*
worry	*Sorge*
worth considering	*eine Überlegung wert*

TEN DEADLY SINS   Chapter 9

TEN DEADLY SINS

- ✱ **OUR STORY: Small talk with a ghost**
- Ⓢ **Small talk SKILLS:**   Avoid the ten deadly sins
- Ⓐ **Small talk AWARENESS:** Identifying deadly sins
- Ⓕ **Small talk PLUS:**   Take a stand and disagree
- Ⓕ **FOCUS:**   Develop your verbal and vocal skills

Time for a smile

Small talk the Finnish way
Two old Finnish friends meet up for a drink after a "long-time-no-see". There's a long but comfortable silence, which lasts for some ten minutes. Then one of the Finns looks up and says: "Well, how are you Matti?" To which Matti replies: "Look, did we come here to talk or to drink?"

Small talk with a ghost

Von Brausewitz is having a last glass of excellent claret (for those of you who don't know it's a dry, red wine) by himself in a quiet, dark corner of the castle library. He ought to feel good but is somehow depressed about the day. Suddenly he becomes aware of a figure sitting in a dark corner. "How come I didn't notice her?" he puzzled. "And, by the way, what a strangely attractive girl!"

In the library, Brausy (**B**), the White Lady (**L**)

B: Excuse me, I didn't see you sitting there. May I offer you a glass of this fine claret?

L: (*in a pleasant melodious voice*) Thank you, no. I neither eat nor drink nowadays. I have no need of worldly pleasures.

B: My God, I must be drunk. Are you trying to tell me you're a ghost?

L: You may call me as you like. I am no longer of your world. To you I appear as a thing of beauty since you yourself are not yet corrupt. To others I appear ugly. It depends on one's character.

B: (*swallowing a whole glass of claret in one gulp*) I don't believe all this. Come off it! There are no such things as ghosts.

L: I am the White Lady of the Castles. I move between castles where there is misery. I am here now. And you have caused this misery.

B: Me? Madam, I'm afraid there must be a misunderstanding.

L: You have misused a fellow human being. You have not noticed the pain of another. You have even exploited the situation for your personal gains and profit.

B: With respect, I see it differently. I assure you it was all fair business with Sir Anthony today.

L: You did not listen to him. Perhaps you will listen to me now. Or you may suffer later.

B: Oh dear me! What have I done that is so bad?

L: Think back! You were a complete "switch-off". Poor Anthony, in despair at losing his home, hoped to discuss with you how to reduce something of his bad luck. You had no ear for him.

B: I'm sorry but I don't agree with you. After all I was interested in his fishing, wasn't I?

L: Yes, but you were deaf and egotistical. And rather than let him pour his heart out, you spoke a monologue about golf and fishing, things he may never do again. Not listening was your first sin, talking too much your second. Your main sin was insensitivity.

B: To be honest, I can't agree with you. Perhaps you're seeing this all a bit too black.

L: And fourth, although he was upset you tried to get free advice for your own ends. You gave Sir Anthony no chance to speak. You interrupted him a thousand times.

B: Well, maybe three or four times.

L: This time you will receive my help. When you open your briefcase tomorrow morning you will find a parchment with the small-talker's complete list of deadly sins. If you dare to sin against the rules of decency again, this parchment will change into a tablet of stone and I'll appear in the shape of the Green Skeleton of Loch Ness, wrap the tablet round your ungrateful neck and throw you into the castle lake.

B: Jesus, that sounded like something from Purgatory. Hey madam ... where's she gone? I must have been dreaming, or was I?

 Small talk SKILLS : Avoid the ten deadly sins

When Brausy woke up the following morning the first thing he did was open his briefcase to look for the parchment. And there it was, as the ghost had promised: an old yellowish document with the small-talker's ten deadly sins, written in old-fashioned letters:

Thou shalt not

1. bore people with too many details
2. interrupt them when they talk about their problems
3. boast of your own achievements
4. over-question people in a negative way
5. try to be better than another
6. try to seek free advice at the expense of another
7. refuse to adapt to another's mood
8. be insensitive to your partner's problems
9. evaluate or look down on the lives of others
10. be a bigot in any matter or meeting
    Or you will never succeed in small talk.

85

Ⓐ Small talk AWARENESS

TASK 1: Identifying deadly sins

Here are a few quotations one should not use in a small-talk situation. Each illustrates a small talk sin. Put the right number from page 85 into the box.

If a swamp alligator could talk, it would talk like Tennesse Williams. *Rex Reed*

I can write better plays than any living dancer and dance better than any living playwright. *Cyril Connolly, 1903–1974*

Oscar Wilde: Do you mind if I smoke?
Sarah Bernhardt: I don't care if you burn.

You don't know a woman until you've met her in court. *Norman Mailer*

Lewis Morris (*on being overlooked for the poet laureateship*): It is a conspiracy of silence against me – a conspiracy of silence. What should I do?
Oscar Wilde: Join it.

Women are like elephants to me; they're nice to look at, but I wouldn't want to own one. *W. C. Fields*

Ruth Gordon: (*explaining her latest role*)
The stage is empty. There's no scenery at all. In the first scene I'm standing on the left side of the stage and the audience has to imagine that I'm eating dinner in a restaurant. Then in scene two, I'm running to the right side of the stage and the audience imagines that I'm in the drawing room.
George S. Kaufmann: And the second night you have to imagine that there is an audience out front.

René B. phoned a former student who was a well-known psychiatrist "Doctor, I'm having a wonderful holiday on the Bahamas. Please tell me what is wrong."

TASK 2: Two more deadly sins

Can you find them?

When Mr Hiram B. Otis, the American Minister, bought Canterville Castle, Lord Canterville himself felt it his duty to mention the fact that there was a ghost when it came to discussing the selling price with Mr Otis.

"We have not cared to live in the place ourselves" said the Lord, "since my grand-aunt, the Dowager Duchess of Bolton, was frightened into a fit, from which she never really recovered, by two skeleton hands being placed on her shoulders as she was dressing for dinner, and I feel bound to tell you, Mr. Otis, that the ghost has been seen by several living members of my family, as well as by the rector of the parish, the Reverend Augustus Dampier, who is a Fellow of King's College, Cambridge. After the unfortunate accident to the Duchess, none of our younger servants would stay with us, and Lady Canterville often got very little sleep at night in consequence of the mysterious noises that came from the corridor and the library."

"My Lord," answered the Minister, "I will take the furniture and the ghost at a valuation. I come from a modern country, where we have everything that money can buy; and with all our young fellows carrying off your best actresses and prima-donnas, I reckon that if there were such a thing as a ghost in Europe, we'd have it at home in a very short time in one of our public museums, or on the road as a show."

"I fear that the ghost exists," said Lord Canterville, smiling. "It has been well known for three centuries, since 1584 in fact, and always makes its appearance before the death of any member of our family."

"Well, so does the family doctor for that matter, Lord Canterville. But there is no such thing, sir, as a ghost, and I guess the laws of Nature are not going to be suspended for the British aristocracy."

(*a dark cloud appeared over the castle and a clap of thunder was heard*)

"What a monstrous climate!" said the American Minister calmly. "I guess the old country is so overpopulated that they haven't enough decent weather for everybody. I have always been of opinion that emigration is the only thing for England."

Small talk PLUS : Take a stand and disagree

Did you notice how Brausy disagreed with the ghost? Most English people are less direct than Germans. They prepare their partners for a disagreement to soften the shock. They use opening phrases like:

I'm afraid ...	*Leider; ich fürchte ...*
Frankly, ...	*Ehrlich gesagt, ...*
To be honest, ...	*Um ehrlich zu sein, ...*
In fact, ...	*Tatsächlich; eigentlich ...*
With respect, ...	*Bei allem Respekt, ...*

TASK 3: Disagreeing politely

Brausy got his opening phrases right. Still, a native speaker might have softened his disagreement even more by adding words like:

... quite ... a slight ... a little ...

To be honest, I can't .... agree with you.
With respect, I see it .... differently.
I'm sorry, I don't .... agree with you. After all ...
I'm afraid there must be .... misunderstanding.

TASK 4: Match them

Match the friendly, neutral and strong phrases of disagreement.

1 I see what you mean, although ...

2 With due respect, what you are saying is impossible.

3 I'm afraid I can't see your point there.

a We'll have to agree to differ.

b I don't disagree altogether. Still ...

c To be quite frank, you're completely mistaken.

F FOCUS : Develop your verbal and vocal skills

In normal face-to-face dialogue research has shown that communication is:

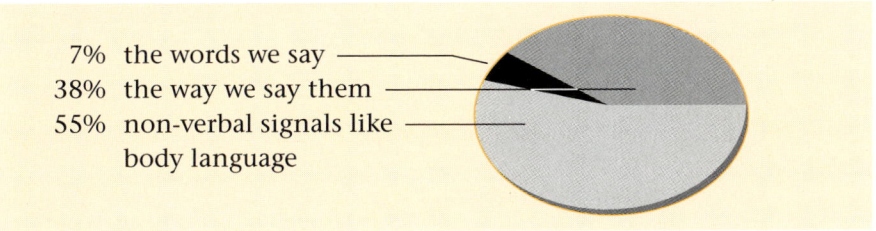

7% the words we say

38% the way we say them

55% non-verbal signals like
body language

It's like in marketing: The package is more important than the contents. Your small talk partners pick up only 7% of a message by paying attention to what you say. The quality of your voice, intonation and stress carry about five times more information than your words. The rest consists of non-verbal signals (see page 94). It's like in an opera: You don't need to understand the text to enjoy the aria. Your voice is the music that accompanies the five "E"s as you enjoy, encourage, exchange, explore, establish and expand through small talk (see page 15). Do you know what it sounds like? Read this page into your tape recorder. Most people are shocked when they listen to their voice for the first time: *That's not me!* What can you do to sound pleasant like the Lady of the Castles?

▶ Deepen your voice. Relax and breathe out so that your vocal cords vibrate gently. They should produce a sound that is one whole tone deeper than your normal pitch.

▶ Find the right speed. Radio announcers read about 150 words a minute. The average rate is about 100 to 130 words a minute, that will do the trick. Vary the speed according to the nature of your talk.

▶ Don't speak like a robot. Emphasise keywords. Move up and down the scale, otherwise your monotonous voice will bore the audience.

▶ Don't use abstract words. Try to paint pictures with your voice. Instead of "nice landscape" say "a clear blue sky, warm sunshine and trees gently swaying in the breeze."

 **WORD AID** AID

bigot	*Rechthaber; religiöser, politischer, patriotischer Eiferer, Frömmler*
bound; feel ~ to	*sich verpflichtet fühlen, zu ...*
clap of thunder	*Donnerschlag*
court	*Gericht*
deadly sin	*Todsünde*
deaf	*taub*
decency	*Anstand, Schicklichkeit*
egotistical	*ichbezogen*
emphasise	*betonen*
ends; for one's own ~	*für seine eigenen Zwecke, Ziele*
evaluate	*beurteilen, bewerten*
expense; at the ~ of	*auf Kosten von*
exploit	*ausnutzen*
gain	*Gewinn*
gulp	*Schluck*
imagine	*sich vorstellen*
insensitivity	*Gefühllosigkeit*
misuse	*missbrauchen*
mood	*Stimmung*
overpopulated	*übervölkert*
parchment	*Pergament*
parish	*Pfarrei*
pitch	*Stimmlage, Stimmhöhe*
poet laureate	*Hofdichter*
Purgatory	*Fegefeuer*
puzzle	*rätseln; Rätsel*
recover	*sich erholen*
reduce	*verringern*
skeleton	*Skelett*
stress	*hier: Betonung*
suffer	*leiden*
sway	*schaukeln, sich wiegen*
upset; be ~	*verärgert sein*
valuation	*hier: Schätzpreis*
vocal cords	*Stimmbänder*
vocal skills	*stimmliche Fertigkeiten*

✳	**OUR STORY: Getting it right at the customer's site**	
⟳	**Small talk SKILLS:**	The fourth **E**
		Body language
Ⓐ	**Small talk AWARENESS:**	Identifying small talk skills
		Small talk etiquette
✛	**Small talk PLUS:**	Toasts
Ⓕ	**FOCUS:**	Exploring future business opportunities

Time for a smile

Talking about others

A gossip talks about others, a bore talks about himself and a brilliant small-talker talks about you.

He was a great patriot, a humanitarian, a loyal friend – provided of course he is really dead. *Voltaire*

Getting it right at the customer's site

Von Brausewitz had a hangover on the next day. He had a quick breakfast and left. Sir Anthony was nowhere to be seen. Obviously the business had fallen through. No point in hanging around. Well, the office would certainly not be happy about that. Two weeks later he was commissioned to visit Scotland; to be exact Gilmore Estate in Perth. So it had finally happened. He was off to see Emily's father.

Lord John Gilmore (**G**), Fritz von Brausewitz (**B**)

B: Thank you very much for a quite remarkable dinner. Your choice of everything was perfect.

G: I'm glad you appreciated it.

B: I've always felt that Scotland offers the best of so many things – fishing, fish itself, fresh air, magnificent mountains, great hiking.[1]

G: I absolutely agree. Perhaps you've noticed that picture on the wall. It's of the Outer Hebrides off the west coast.

B: When I think back to the Hebrides it wasn't so much the hiking as the trout fishing. Great times. Were you on the island of Uist?

G: Yes, I stayed at the hotel in the bay, the Black Duck, very much old world charm.[2] (*Sound of bottle opening*)

B: I stayed there, too, for my trout fishing. Great atmosphere! But, Sir, perhaps you'd like to discuss the matter of Gilmore Estate, if you feel like it.[3]

G: Certainly, Mr von Brausewitz. Well, I'm basically in a quandary about what to do. I'm in two minds whether to sell. You know my daughter and myself have spent so many beautiful years here.

B: Well, if you sold, you'd certainly have a large quantity of free capital. You could live a less stressful life. Perhaps a trip round the world and you could then settle somewhere in a small villa in London.[4]

G: I'm afraid you can't transplant an old tree.

B: Well, you wouldn't have to worry about managing the estate and involving your daughter.

G: Ah yes, my daughter. You're acquainted with her, are you not? What has she told you about this matter?

B: She was most tactful. I think she would prefer not to leave.

G: I guessed so. But, von Brausewitz, how can I solve this problem? I'm at my wits' end.

B: (*standing up, pacing: He looks Lord Gilmore in the eyes in a friendly way but directly*)[5] Lord Gilmore, I believe I may have a solution which is a positive compromise for all sides. (*Brausy sits and draws his chair towards Lord Gilmore*)[6]

G: What's your proposal?

B: (*speaking more slowly*) Your estate is the answer. Look, if I may show you an outline map. You see this area here. Fifty acres or more, part of the river running through, and the gatekeeper's lodge. Perhaps we can make an arrangement to purchase this slice. That would leave you with ... (*fade out*)

G: (*fade in*) Very impressive, very impressive, my boy. You seem to have saved Gilmore Castle for the generations to come. I appreciate your suggestion very much since I'm aware of the fact that your company would have liked to buy the entire estate. Let's raise our glasses to our future contract.

B: Cheers! ... By the way Lord Gilmore, you seem to be the most well-connected person I know. That reminds me, you don't happen to know any castle-owners to whom I could offer my services?[7]

G: I'm afraid that there are quite a few poor devils who are in a similar predicament to mine. I'll keep my ears to the ground.

B: And I'll see to it that the company pays you a fair price. Feel free to call me up any time when you have a question about the details.

 **Small talk SKILLS**

1. The fourth E: Exploring future business opportunities

You remember the first four "E"s?

1. Enjoy the moment and the company (chapter 5)
2. Encourage others to participate (chapter 6)
3. Exchange information and ideas with others (chapter 7)

In this dialogue Brausy has reached the level of the fourth E:

4. Explore future business opportunities

2. Body language: Our BEHAVE-Formula

You will never get a second chance to make a good impression. The first 30 minutes are the most important ones. You are already talking with your body by the way you dress, move, sit, stand and walk before you speak a word. And there is the facial expression, the tone of your voice, the distance you keep: everything contributes to the way we communicate with another non-verbally. Our BEHAVE-Formula helps you to remember the six golden rules of body language:

B **Body:** Lean forward to encourage, lean or move away to discourage your partner to continue.

E **Eyes:** Don't stare at your partner. Keep eye contact for about 3 to 5 seconds before you look away. Glance down to the side and then back at your partner's face.

H **Head:** Nod from time to time. It is a signal that you are listening and enjoying the conversation. A smile conveys warmth.
Hands: Raise a finger to signal that you want to comment.

A **Appearance:** You are what you wear. Your clothes are part of your body and speak a language of their own.
Attention: Direct your attention to your partner. Don't fold your arms across your chest; this creates a barrier.

V **Voice:** Breathe in through your nose and take in warmed air. Speak in a calm, low voice at a rate of 100 to 120 words per minute.

E **Ease:** Relax! Stand at ease and be at ease. It will make your partner feel comfortable. Keep a distance of at least one arm's length. When the conversation gets more personal you may move in up to 40–50 centimetres.

Food for thought

Talk low, talk slow, and don't say too much.
John Wayne (1907–1979)

Don't talk anything you can smile, don't smile anything you can wink, don't wink anything you can nod.
Earl Long, American politician (1895–1960)

Better to remain silent and be thought a fool than to speak out and remove all doubt. *Abraham Lincoln*

Ⓐ Small talk AWARENESS

TASK 1: | **Identifying small talk skills**

We have numbered some small talk skills in the dialogue. Can you put the numbers next to the skills? The first has been done for you.

He unlocks memories to meet on common ground.	2
He uses distance to signal the change in the conversation.	
He uses body language to prepare an important proposal.	
He wants to win a network partner.	
He is sensitive and lets Lord Gilmore choose the topic.	
Brausy compliments Lord Gilmore indirectly.	
He plays the devil's advocate to provoke a decision.	

TASK 2: | **Small talk etiquette**

You remember our IMPACT-Formula (if not see page 33):
Integrity, **M**anners, **P**ersonality, **A**ppearance, **C**onsideration, **T**act

Here are a few quotations from small-talkers who have sinned against IMPACT. Put the first letter next to the right quotation. The first has been done for you.

Don't misunderstand me – my dislike for you is purely platonic. *Herbert Beerbohm Tree*	T
When I want a peerage, I shall buy one like an honest man. *Lord Northcliffe*	
One should never be unnecessarily rude to a lady except in streetcars. *O. Henry*	
The louder he talked of his honour, the faster we counted our spoons. *R.W. Emerson*	
I'd rather eat shit than wear a suit. *Bill Carter*	
I much prefer travelling on British ships. There's none of that nonsense about women and children first. *Somerset Maugham*	

 **Small talk PLUS : Toasts**

You are at a party and nobody takes any notice of you. What can you do?
Well, why don't you raise your glass to your neighbour, smile and say:

Cheers!
Good health!
To your good health!

If he or she is an educated person they will follow your example. But what
to say next? Introduce yourself and make a comment on the situation:

Nice party, isn't it?
How long have you known the host? etc.

There are of course more formal occasions when you can raise your glass.
A toast is a nice conclusion to a successful negotiation, a signature under a
contract, a wedding or at the end of an after-dinner speech.

TASK 3: Let's practise toasts

raise		wish		celebrate
	make a toast		toast	
propose		here's		bottoms
	future		luck	

1. ..... to the beautiful bride.
2. I want to .... the best for the newly wed couple.
3. I rise to ..... our Japanese guests.
4. I'd like to .... to our new colleague.
5. Let's ..... our glasses to the future of Gilmore Castle.
6. I'd like to .... a toast to the conclusion of our contract.
7. Best of ....., you two. And now everybody, ...
8. Gentlemen, let's ...... this with a glass of champagne.

(F) FOCUS : Exploring future business opportunities

As a small-talker you are not only interested in other people. You have your agenda of "What I want to get" in mind. In the course of your conversation with the right person, to whom you have been politely listening for a while, you try to expand the conversation and enter into professional areas.

You seem to know a lot about these things.	*Sie scheinen eine Menge darüber zu wissen.*
Is this one of your hobbies?	*Ist das eines Ihrer Hobbys?*
You seem to be an expert on ...	*Sie scheinen ein Experte in ... zu sein.*
You must have a lot of experience with ...	*Sie müssen viel Erfahrung haben mit ...*

Don't confuse interest with curiosity. You ask questions to explore common ground. But remember that questions about a person's professional background are only polite if you have introduced yourself.

Do you do this for a living?	*Tun Sie das beruflich?*
What profession are you in?	*Was machen Sie beruflich?*
Where can I get more information about ...?	*Wo kann ich mehr Informationen über ... erhalten?*

This is the moment when you can find out about the other small-talker's jobs or hobbies.

By the way, I'm a lawyer. Does there happen to be a colleague at the table?	*Übrigens, ich bin Rechtsanwalt. Ist zufällig ein Kollege mit am Tisch?*

This might be an encouragement for others to come out themselves and exchange business cards – because you never know when they might come in handy. "These chaps have everything to sell and to buy." That is what most business people think who are on the lookout for opportunities. The least you can get from a small talk situation like this is better service.

What to say when the time has come

You are the best-connected person I know. That reminds me, you don't happen to know a good address for ...	*Ich kenne niemanden mit besseren Verbindungen als Sie. Dabei fällt mir ein, kennen Sie zufällig eine gute Adresse für ...?*
By the way, if you come across someone who has a castle to sell, please let me know.	*Übrigens, wenn Sie jemanden treffen, der ein Schloss zu verkaufen hat, lassen Sie es mich bitte wissen.*
Obviously our business interests overlap in some areas. I think we can learn from each other.	*Unsere Geschäftsinteressen scheinen sich zu überlappen. Ich glaube, wir können voneinander lernen.*

Small talk with a purpose

A conversation such as the following is often a follow-up to a small talk situation.

A: I'd like to invite you for a drink, if you can spare a minute?

B: To what do I owe this honour?

A: I'd like to get to know you better because I noticed we have something in common.

B: What might that be?

A: Well, you mentioned that your company manufactures electrical vehicles. We produce a new type of speed control device for these vehicles that saves a lot of energy.

B: Hmm ... that could be interesting. I've got to warn you, though, that we have long-term contracts with our suppliers.

A: Well, one day you might be developing a new model. May I send you my brochure?

B: What's the name of your company?

A: Bush Electronics. We are a young enterprise, not exactly the market leader, but we have a team of creative research engineers.

B: We are certainly interested in new developments in our field. Send me your brochure, but I can't promise anything.

WORD AID

acquainted with	bekannt sein mit; vertraut sein mit
acre	1 hectare ≈ 2.47 acres
appreciate	schätzen, mögen
behave	sich benehmen
bore	Langweiler; Ekel
Cheers!	Prost!
chest	Brust
choice	Wahl
commission	beauftragen; Kommission
conclusion	Abschluss; Schlussfolgerung
confuse	verwechseln
contribute	beitragen
convey	bedeuten, mitteilen
curiosity	Neugier
ease; stand at ~	bequem, entspannt stehen
entire; the ~ estate	das ganze Anwesen
expand	ausdehnen, erweitern
explore	erkunden
facial expression	Gesichtsausdruck
glance down	nach unten blicken
gossip	Klatsch; Klatschbase
handy; come in ~	gelegen kommen
hang around	verweilen
hangover	Kater (den man sitzen hat)
hiking	Wandern
humanitarian	Menschenfreund
involve someone	jemanden heranziehen
lean forward	sich vorbeugen
long-term contracts	langfristige Verträge
magnificent	großartig, herrlich, prächtig
minds; be in two ~	hin- und hergerissen sein
nod	nicken
opportunity	Gelegenheit
pace	(auf und ab) schreiten

peerage	*Adelsstand, Peerswürde*
predicament	*Notlage*
prefer	*vorziehen, lieber tun*
proposal	*Vorschlag*
provided	*vorausgesetzt*
purchase	*kaufen; Kauf*
quandary	*Dilemma, Verlegenheit*
raise; let's ~ our glasses!	*erheben wir unsere Gläser!*
remind someone of	*jemanden erinnern an*
research	*Forschung*
rude	*unhöflich, grob*
saved	*retten; sparen*
settle	*sich niederlassen*
site	*Sitz; Gelände*
slice	*Scheibe, Streifen*
spare; can you ~ a minute?	*haben Sie einen Moment Zeit?*
speed control device	*Geschwindigkeitsregler*
spoon	*Löffel*
stare at someone	*jemanden anstarren*
suggestion	*Vorschlag*
toast	*Trinkspruch*
transplant	*verpflanzen*
wedding	*Hochzeit*
wink	*zuzwinkern, blinzeln*
wits; be at one's ~ end	*mit seinem Latein am Ende sein*

Time for a smile

Integrity
The best way to tell if a man is honest is to ask him if he is honest. If he says he is, you know he's a crook.

Those are my principles. If you don't like them I have others.
Groucho Marx

RECOGNISING SMALL TALK SINNERS

Chapter 11

- ✳ **OUR STORY:** Visit to his bankrupt lordship
- ⟳ **Small talk SKILLS:** Introducing a customer
  Pouring oil on troubled waters
  Small talk sinners
- Ⓐ **Small talk AWARENESS:** Recognising small talk sinners
- ➕ **Small talk PLUS:** How to be a schoolmaster
  The polite adviser
- Ⓕ **FOCUS:** From small talk to business

Time for a smile

How to handle boasters

Joe Mushmallow was being driven around London by a taxi driver. As they passed Buckingham Palace Joe asked: "Say, that's not a bad little joint. How long did it take to put that up?" – "A couple of years, I suppose," said the chauffeur. – "Gosh!" said Joe. "We'd have thrown that up in six weeks back home."

Shortly afterwards they passed St. Paul's cathedral.

"Gee, that's elegant. How long did that take to build?"

The Englishman , becoming irritable, said "About three months."

"In America we'd have that up in a month," boasted the American.

Then they drove past the Houses of Parliament.

"Jeepers, what a nice little hut. How long were they working on that?"

The taxi driver sniffed, stared out of the window and said: "Well, it wasn't there when I passed last night."

 **Visit to his bankrupt lordship**

The weeks drifted by. Von Brausewitz began to feel settled in. He was beginning to enjoy himself. He was getting his hand in at fishing, golf and squash and had enjoyed one or two romantic evenings with English roses. The only thing he was still not sure about was his skill in small-talking both in business and in private circles. The English had such sensitive ways of expressing themselves. Anyhow, he just had to be a bit careful. The coming Friday was the next big occasion. Brausy was to support negotiations between Joe Mushmallow from Texas and the Earl of Chutsworth House in Nottinghamshire. The Earl was being forced to sell up. Same old story. What with extra taxes and maintaining the large property, he had found himself unable to pay.

Earl of Chutsworth (**C**), Joe Mushmallow (**M**),
Fritz von Brausewitz (**B**)

B: So, here we all are together to inspect the property. This is the Earl of Chutsworth, Sir, this is Mr Mushmallow from the United States of America.

M: That's it, Brausy. You hit the nail right on the head. From the centre of the very earth, the world of black gold and money, Texas.[1]

C: Well, I'm very pleased to make your acquaintance, I'm sure.

M: I just bet you are. You'd better get a few of those oil dollars to dig you and your cabin out of the quicksand.[2]

C: Well, I'm certain you have enough of them in your country to compensate the lack of other things such as …

M: (*interrupting*) Money makes up for everything. It allows you to live the way you want, doesn't it? Which is what you can't do, I guess, your lordship. Name me a problem that money can't solve. It's obvious, isn't it![3]

B: Perhaps we should leave the financial discussions until later. Let's look through the property, shall we? (*sound of door shutting*)

B: This is a most charming room with carved wooden walls.

C: Yes, and I dearly hope they will all be taken care of and respected by the next owner. It breaks my heart to part with it all.

B: I'm sure any new owner would fall in love with it at first sight.

M: Never mind break your heart! I'm damn sure it'll repair your pockets. Ha ha ha![2]

C: I beg your pardon. I don't ...

M: (*interrupting*) You know, your lordship, what you should do is make a plan. Think what assets you've got, reckon out how you can put them to use. See what profit you can make. Why don't you get yourself a financial advisor?[4]

C: Different people have different values. And in my case I ...

M: (*interrupting again*) Damn it! I see red when I hear that word "values". Back in good old Texas we have a lot of damned socialists. They have values. But when you look close at them they're all lazy good-for-no-things who can't hold down a job. They are all in line at the employment office. Stealing the money from those who really earn it. I'd throw the whole bunch of them in jail.[5]

B: Gentlemen, my dear gentlemen. Let's agree to differ on those sensitive political matters. I think we're all agreed this is a marvellous building that we're standing in.

M: Well, you're certainly right there, fella. And it'll look even finer being taken care of and respected over there in the US.

C: You mean you want to transplant it?

M: Yes sir, bricks, panes and mortar. Mere child's play for our engineers.[1] Why are you staring at me? We aren't talking about the Empire State Building, are we? (*fade out*)

Small talk SKILLS

1. Introducing a customer

Did Brausy get the introductions right? Shouldn't he have introduced the younger American to the higher-ranking Earl first? No! When introducing a customer treat the customer as the superior. Say his name first to honour the business relationship.

2. Pouring oil on troubled waters

Sex, politics and firm beliefs are tricky subjects that you may discuss with close friends but not with strangers. Brausy did well to lead the conversation back to business: *Let's agree to differ on those sensitive political matters. I think we're all agreed this is a marvellous building that we're standing in.*

3. Small talk sinners: Missionaries, Schoolmasters, Bigots and Boasters

The Missionary knows all the answers. He tries to convert his partners to his point of view. What he wants is confirmation, not conversation. He does not keep an open mind, he seeks to change everybody's mind. He is a bad listener and a boring small-talker.

The Schoolmaster is a bad small-talker, too. He is generous with good advice nobody has asked for. It seems to be a typical West German quality. That is why after the reunification our fellow countrymen in the new eastern "Länder" nick-named the West Germans "Besser Wessis". (see **Small talk plus**)

The Bigot: East – West, his country is best. You remember Hiram B. Otis, the American minister who bought Canterville Castle? He is the harmless patriot, the bigot who has a simple explanation for everything. Joe Mushmallow, on the other hand, is the unpleasant bigot with tunnel vision: "unemployed people are lazy, Russians are communists, immigrants are parasites". Instead of a considered opinion of his own, he has prejudices.

The Boaster insists on one-upmanship. He has the faster car, the bigger house and the brighter children. If you talk about skiing at the Zugspitze he tops it with his expedition to the Nanga Parbat. If you win a small sum at the lottery, he tells you how he made a fortune on the stock exchange.

You might have realised that Joe Mushmallow personifies all four characters, which makes him the perfect bore.

Time for a smile

One-upmanship
That evening Joe Mushmallow was invited to the home of Earl of Chutsworth. The host and his wife were playing a delicate duet on their grand piano. He listened for a while and then said: "That's nice. Very nice. But back home, me and my baby, we have a piano each."

Joe Mushmallow was visiting a zoo in London. In front of the kangaroo house he stopped dead. Still chewing his chewing gum he said to a bystander: "One thing I really grant you Brits. Your grasshoppers are really a lot bigger than ours back in Texas."

Small talk AWARENESS

TASK 1: Recognising small talk sinners

In the dialogue we have numbered some small talk sins which illustrate more or less the behaviour of the perfect bore. Can you put the numbers into the right-hand column?

The Missionary
The Schoolmaster
The Bigot
The Boaster
The Insensitive

Small talk PLUS

How to be a schoolmaster

Schoolmasters always try to show you the path of virtue. They give their piece of advice without being asked for help.

What you should do is make a plan.
Why don't you get yourself a financial advisor?
If I were you I would take a few driving lessons.
It's high time you did something about your body.
I think you'd better consult a psychiatrist.
You ought to be more careful with money.

The polite adviser

He asks whether his advice is welcome or offers his advice in an indirect way.

Would you like to hear what I did in that situation?
I was wondering what I would do in your situation.
Don't you think it might be a good idea to consult a financial adviser?

F **FOCUS** : **From small talk to business**

Here is a true story about how small talk without a purpose can result in unexpected benefits. It actually happened at the bar of my last holiday club on the Canaries. I – one of your authors – was preparing this book and had some reason to observe small-talkers on holiday.

One day I was listening to two gentlemen who, in the course of their conversation, found out that they had both studied law and economics at the same university. The elder was the owner of a well-known firm of consultants, a success coach, as he called himself. The younger was planning to leave his bank and become self-employed. At the end of an evening of small talk the younger was invited to attend one of his expensive three-day seminars in Frankfurt – for free.

We had some habits in common, the success coach and I. We would meet in the swimming pool early in the morning and go for a jog afterwards. In the afternoons, we would meet in the sauna and talked about our weight problems and what to do about it. We both had a seminar to prepare – sufficient common ground to engage in small talk.

He told me he did seminars in France and was going to do seminars in San Francisco the following year. He and his team had to brush up their English in a very short time. I told him that we were writing books for a business English series. He was interested and I had to promise to fax him the list of our publications. When I mentioned that my partner and co-author did customised crash courses he became even more interested in keeping in touch.

The following day he told me during one of our jogs that he had a standing order with his book shop. They supplied him with the latest management books as soon as they appeared on the market. There was only one problem. Most of them were in English and he was looking for somebody to do eight to ten page abstracts in German. Would we be willing to do that for him? All these opportunities were the result of enjoyable small talk situations without a purpose.

In a fax he let me know that he had bought most of our books in the business series and that he and his team planned to come to Heidelberg to combine an English crash course and a seminar in speed-reading which a colleague at my school specialises in. We'll see whether these prospects will materialise.

WORD AID

abstract	*Zusammenfassung*
acquaintance	*Bekanntschaft*
advisor	*Berater*
assets	*Aktiva, Vermögenswerte*
attend a seminar	*an einem Seminar teilnehmen*
boast	*prahlen*
bore	*Ekel, Langweiler*
brick	*Ziegelstein*
brush up	*aufpolieren*
carved wooden walls	*geschnitzte Holztäfelungen*
confirmation	*Bestätigung*
considered opinion	*wohl überlegte Meinung*
convert	*bekehren*
customised courses	*maßgeschneiderte Kurse*
duet; play a ~ on the piano	*vierhändig spielen*
economics	*Volkswirtschaft*
fella (fellow)	*Kumpel*
fortune	*Vermögen*
get one's hand in	*in Übung kommen*
grasshopper	*Heuschrecke*
insure	*versichern*
irritable	*gereizt*
jail	*Gefängnis, Kittchen*
joint	*hier: Schuppen, Hütte*
labour exchange	*Arbeitsamt*
lack	*Mangel*
law	*Jura*
lazy good-for-nothing	*fauler Taugenichts*
maintain	*instand halten*
marvellous	*herrlich*
mortar	*Mörtel*
nick-name	*einen Spitznamen geben*
pane	*Fensterscheibe*
part with	*sich trennen von*

path of virtue	*Pfad der Tugend*
personify	*verkörpern*
prospects	*Aussichten*
put something up	*errichten, aufbauen*
quicksand	*Treibsand*
reunification	*Wiedervereinigung*
seek	*suchen*
settled in; feel ~ ~	*sich heimisch fühlen*
speed-reading	*Schnelllesen*
standing order	*Dauerauftrag*
stock exchange	*Börse*
stop dead	*plötzlich stehen bleiben*
sufficient	*ausreichend*
superior	*Höhergestellte(r), Vorgesetzte(r)*
top something	*etwas übertreffen*
transplant	*versetzen, verpflanzen*
tricky subjects	*gefährliche, kitzlige Themen*
troubled waters	*hier: erhitzte Gemüter*
tunnel vision	*Scheuklappen aufhaben*
value	*Wert*
weight	*Gewicht*

Time for a smile

What to say ...
... to a schoolmaster
I'm not young enough to know everything.
Sir James Barrie (author of Peter Pan)

... to a boaster
Anonymous singer: You know, my dear, I insured my voice for
                   fifty thousand dollars.
Miriam Hopkins: That's wonderful. And what did you do
                   with the money?

NETWORK IN THE FOURTH DIMENSION

Chapter 12

- (✳) **OUR STORY:** Interviewing a ghost
- (S) **Small talk SKILLS:** Unlocking memories
  The ADAM-Formula
  The fifth E: Establishing a network
  The SELL-Formula
- (A) **Small talk AWARENESS:** Using the ADAM-Formula
- (P) **Small talk PLUS:** Ending a small talk
  Creating links
- (F) **FOCUS:** The importance of the fifth **E**
  Two case studies

Time for a smile

How to be a bore

A bore is fellow who, when you ask him the time, starts telling you how watches are made.

A bore is someone to whom you should never say "Hallo, how are you?" He will spend an hour telling you.

✳ Interviewing a ghost

Von Brausewitz and Mushmallow stayed the night at Chutsworth House. The evening was dark and stormy. Von Brausewitz retired to bed early with a small carafe of exquisite Spanish brandy, Duc d'Alba. There were some perks to his job after all. He was sitting by the fireside. Suddenly the curtains flapped about unexpectedly. He looked over to them. When he glanced back to the fire the strange lady's eyes met his:

The White Lady of the Castles (**L**), von Brausewitz (**B**)

B: (*startled*) Ach, du meine Güte. It's you again. So you weren't a dream.

L: I'm what you see before you.

B: Well, you don't frighten me any more. I'd like to know a little more about you. Do you mind talking about it, I mean would you mind telling me how you ... eh ... died?

L: It's of no matter. Those times are past and now time has no meaning for me. I lived in Shardlow Castle in Derbyshire. It was the eve of my marriage to the Sheriff of Nottingham. I was walking towards the main hall in the castle. It was a stormy night like tonight. The storm was so powerful that it dislodged a stone from the castle wall. It fell down onto me. At least that's the official version. Anyway, I was smashed to pieces. Well, they gave me a most pompous burial. I was among the mourners. King John, the scoundrel, was there, too, and ...

B: (*interrupting*) Goodness me! I'm so sorry. I'm touched. I don't know what to say. How long have you been, well, haunting castles around Britain?

L: Oh, it seems like a long, long time but it's quite recently that I left my physical body. Perhaps 600 years ago.

B: My God! That's centuries ago. Around 1400.

L: No matter! History. Although I always turn green when I think of those hypocrites at my burial.

B: You mentioned King John. You don't – or should I say, didn't seem to like him particularly.

L: Well, I should have scared him to death at the burial. Storms do not dislodge stones from British castle walls, if you know what I mean.

Let's not talk about the past. But I have a present for you. It is a present for your future.

B: I must say I'm honoured.

L: You have a noble heart. But you are following the wrong path. You go to castles in misery, where the old families and their histories are forced to disappear because of financial problems at a difficult time.

B: That's right. Castles have little place in modern England. But help me to understand why you keep appearing to a German salesman, a foreigner like me.

L: You help to put the families out of house and home, although your heart is not in it. You can stop this. Try another way!

B: Excuse me, try what?

L: Go to the castles and offer your knowledge and assistance so that the families may stay in their homes. Your knowledge of working with money can help. You can advise.

B: But advise who? How can I know where to ...

L: (*interrupting*) When there is misery in a castle I will know about it. And when I know I will come to you. I can reach you in any castle.

B: It's been fascinating talking to you about the past and the future. So you are telling me to be a consultant to castle-owners and you'll let me know where and when? And I should give up my job? Well, I must say I'm intrigued by all this. I'm looking forward to meeting you again. ... Oh, where's she gone? My God, what a damn fool I am. Talking to myself.

 **Small talk SKILLS**

1. Unlocking memories

Do you remember where you came across this technique first? Memories of childhood, school, one's first job etc. are experiences we have in common with everybody who is not a ghost. It is a direct way of getting to know people. However, don't unlock unpleasant memories about death and dying when your partner is an ordinary human being. Simply change the subject.

2. Soft interviewing: The ADAM-Formula

Here we give you a short overview of four questioning techniques: In the first task we will ask you to identify these question types in the dialogue.

A About	When in doubt ask "about". *Tell me more about ...?* At the beginning of a conversation to get the partner talking, to hear his or her attitudes or beliefs.
D Drill	*How old were you at that time?* When the partner is rambling or talking too much, when you wish to "drill" for more facts or details.
A Aid	*How can I help? Which castle-owners?* After vague statements questions ask for help, for precise instruction, missing links, facts or details.
M Mirror	*You seem to be upset with ...? If I understood you correctly you ...? In other words you don't ...?* Like a mirror the questions are reflected to your partner. The psychologist uses this technique when people are getting emotionally involved or when he doesn't wish to influence them.

3. The fifth E: Establishing a network

Networks develop out of small talk situations. Networking is small-talking with the purpose of getting to know the right people who know the right people. The experienced small-talker creates a web of agents that inform him about business opportunities. In our dialogue the ghost made a successful attempt to win her first network partner. More about that in our **Focus section**.

4. Ending a conversation with the SELL-Formula

Small talk with a purpose in mind means self-marketing, selling yourself to your best advantage. Whereas the first impression you make is the most important, the last impression in a small talk situation is the most profitable because it deepens the relationship and can build a bridge for later.

How do you quit a conversation? "Well, I'm afraid it's time for me to leave. I'll see you later" is not a good way of creating lasting links. That's where our SELL-Formula might come in handy. Brausy got it right this time, didn't he?

S-um up	Go back to the beginning and summarise what was important for you. *So what we have agreed on is ...* Give positive feedback: *It's been good talking to you.*
E-xplain	Explain the next step. Say what you will do next or what you want your partner to do. *So you expect me to ... and you'll let me know ...*
L-ink	Create links. If there is no next step to take, think about how to continue the relationship. *I'll get back to you next week. I'll send you the article about ... I hope we can do business some day.*
L-eave	Know when to quit, don't overstay your welcome. Shake hands and leave.

A) Small talk AWARENESS

TASK 1: Using the ADAM-Formula

Here are some questions Brausy asked the ghost. Can you put the right number into the table?

1. How long have you been, well, haunting castles around Britain?
2. I'd like to know a little more about you if you're willing to tell me.
3. You mentioned King John. You don't – or should I say, didn't seem to like him particularly, did you?
4. Try what? What do you mean by "help them"? But advise who?

Question	No
A-bout question	
D-rill question	
A-id question	
M-irror question	

 **Small talk PLUS**

1. Ending a small talk

What Brausy might have said to the ghost:

It's been so good to talk to someone who is not of this world.
I must say I'm intrigued by all these supernatural things.
Wonderful to talk to someone who is not interested in
worldly pleasures.

TASK 2: Spot the mistake

Here are some more examples. But this time there is a slight mistake in
each sentence for you to correct.

1. I'm so glad you introduced myself to the world of ghosts.
2. It's been fascinating hearing to your memories from the past.
3. It's nice to meet an eyewitness from King John's yard.

2. Creating links

What you can say to establish an network:

Why don't you give me a call? Here's my card.
I hope we can do business some day.
I'd like to spend time with you going over your ideas about ...

TASK 3: More mistakes for you to spot

1. I'm going to send you that article over haunted castles.
2. I'll be thinking of your suggestions over the weekend.
3. I'll get back to you on the weekend to resume our conversation.

FOCUS 1 : The importance of the fifth E

The fifth **E**: Establish and expand your network. It is an age old strategy that has developed in big families and clans. The rule of the game for all members is to help each other unselfishly. This mutual help is still going on in society today, take the Rotary Clubs, Lions Clubs, secret societies, student organisations, sects old and new or the Cosa Nostra. The rules have changed but it is still a game called networking.

▶ Let's face it. In 85 percent of cases a promotion, a job or a contract doesn't go to the best applicant, but to someone else. Who is this "someone else"? It is the better networker. You might have observed this in your company, among your acquaintances or, where it is more common, in politics.

▶ You can look for a better job in adverts. However, about 80 percent of jobs are not advertised. They are either only posted internally, or filled by a friend of a friend or a network partner of a networker. That means that most of the few vacancies advertised are already filled before you even apply.

▶ Several surveys have shown that getting a job through an ad has a less than 7 percent chance of success*. Whereas getting a job through networking rates up to 86 percent. So networking can be up to twelve times more effective than merely answering an advertisement.

In our industrial society the altruistic family structure no longer exists – with the exception of the Mafia. Network partners expect something in return: respect, information, a favour in the future. In a way, networking has replaced the solidarity of the clans. While they pursue the interests of the family as a whole even if they had to sacrifice the interests of the individual member, the network is based on reciprocity. It is a game without losers. The rule is: You scratch my back and I will scratch yours. But how to find the right backs to scratch? In most cases it all starts with small talk. Some of the small-talkers you have met might have been networkers and you were not even aware of it.

---

* Rupert Hart, Effective Networking for Professional Success. Kogan Page, London 1996.

FOCUS 2 : Two case studies

CASE 1 : IQ gets you hired – EQ gets you higher

Richard B. applied for a professorship in English at a German university. He had the most experience, a doctorate, a long list of international publications and he was a native speaker of English on top of it. He had by far the best qualifications of all the other applicants. But the job went to someone else less qualified. Why?

Maybe the successful applicant had one ability that Richard B. had not: superior people skills. In fact, the Stanford Research Institute, Harvard, and the Carnegie Foundation did some research and found that technical skills and knowledge account for only 15 percent of getting a promotion, keeping a job or winning a contract; 85 percent of your success in business has to do with your ability to make the right contacts.

What are these people skills? They have nothing to do with your IQ (intelligence quotient). They have lot to do with your EQ (emotional quotient). "Your intelligence quotient gets you hired, your emotional quotient gets you higher" as the saying goes. And can you hardly improve your IQ whereas emotional attitudes can be changed. Small talk qualities are part of our emotional attitudes towards people. These skills can become part of your EQ. They are necessary for making good contacts that result in good contracts.

CASE 2 : The indirect approach

During my last holiday I was the witness to a very elegant method on how to contact an important person. I was lying in a deckchair at the swimming pool. Next to me was a mother watching her three children. I knew that her husband was an important real estate agent. Suddenly a gentleman walked over to us, introduced himself to the lady and said: "I happened to notice the way your husband was looking after your children yesterday. I just wanted to let you know that I've never seen a father playing with his kids for such a long time."

The lady smiled: "Well, you were lucky. He normally minds the children every second leap year."

That was all. But obviously the young man was counting on the lady to pass the compliment on to her husband. The following day I saw both the gentleman and the real estate agent at the pool, immersed in what seemed to be a serious conversation. I leave the rest to your imagination.

WORD AID

ability	*Fähigkeit*
account for	*erklären*
acquaintance	*Bekannte(r), Bekanntschaft*
advantage	*Vorteil*
advise	*beraten*
aid	*Hilfe; Hilfestellung*
altruistic	*selbstlos*
applicant	*Bewerber*
apply	*sich bewerben*
assistance	*Hilfe, Beistand*
attitude	*Haltung, Einstellung*
aware; be ~ of something	*sich einer Sache bewusst sein*
burial, funeral	*Begräbnis*
century	*Jahrhundert*
count on	*zählen auf, rechnen mit*
curtain	*Vorhang*
deckchair	*Liegestuhl*
dislodge	*(heraus)lösen, lockern*
distribute	*verteilen*
drill	*bohren*
eve	*Vorabend*
fierce; competition is ~	*Wettbewerb ist hart, scharf*
fireside, fireplace	*offener Kamin*
flap about	*in helle Aufregung geraten*
frighten	*erschrecken*
gift	*Gabe*
handy; come in ~	*gelegen kommen*
haunt castles	*in Schlössern spuken*
hypocrite	*Heuchler*
immersed in	*vertieft, versunken in*
influence	*beeinflussen*
involved; emotionally ~	*gefühlsmäßig betroffen*
knowledge	*Wissen, Kenntnis*
leap year	*Schaltjahr*

link; create ~s	*Bande knüpfen*
matter; of no ~	*belanglos*
mention	*erwähnen*
mind the children	*sich um die Kinder kümmern*
mirror	*widerspiegeln*
mutual help	*gegenseitige Hilfe*
observe	*beobachten*
ordinary human being	*gewöhnlicher Sterblicher*
overstay one's welcome	*länger verweilen, als anderen lieb ist*
overview	*Überblick*
perks	*Vergünstigungen, Vorrechte*
promotion	*Beförderung*
pursue the interests of someone	*jemandes Interesse verfolgen*
quit a conversation	*ein Gespräch beenden*
ramble	*ausschweifen*
recently	*kürzlich, neulich*
reciprocity; based on ~	*auf Gegenseitigkeit beruhen*
reflect	*widerspiegeln*
resume a conversation	*ein Gespräch fortsetzen*
retire	*sich zurückziehen*
rule of the game	*Spielregel*
sacrifice	*opfern*
scare someone to death	*jemanden zu Tode erschrecken*
scratch	*kratzen*
startled	*aufgeschreckt*
summarise	*zusammenfassen*
touched	*gerührt*
unlock memories	*Erinnerungen wecken*
watchword	*Parole*
web	*Netz, Geflecht*
whereas	*wohingegen*

SENSE AND SENSITIVITY

Chapter 13

(✱) **OUR STORY: At cross-purposes with the Lady**

(S) **Small talk SKILLS:**   Tough talk versus soft talk
     Monologue versus dialogue

(A) **Small talk AWARENESS:** Deadly sins

(P) **Small talk PLUS:**   Soften your talk
     Emotional Quotient

(F) **FOCUS:**   Small talk at cross-purposes
     IQ versus EQ

Time for a smile

Talking at cross-purposes
Misunderstanding in the clothes' shop:
"I need some underpants."
"How long do you want them?"
"I want to buy them, not to rent them."

"Now that you are married, may I give you some
good advice. Take out some insurance."
"But why? My wife isn't dangerous."

"I've lost my dog."
"If I were you I'd put an advertisement in the paper."
"Rubbish! You seem to forget that my dog can't read."

At cross-purposes with the Lady

Joe Mushmallow felt he had really given that silly old aristocrat a smack on the nose. It was getting late, Joe was sitting on an old terrace in the east wing of the castle. The sun was on the horizon, a deep red line with black clouds. The storm clouds were beginning to dominate the scene. The rain started falling. Joe moved to his chamber with a bottle of sour bourbon whisky. He was tired.

Joe Mushmallow (**M**), a ghost, Lady of the Castle (**L**)

M: Damn these historical misfits. What do they really expect? Hey, who are you? Come out of the shadow. Jesus, what an old witch!

L: I am the Lady of the Castles. At the moment I am in this castle because there is misery here.

M: Castle? You call this a castle? Back home we've got bigger log cabins than this pile of stones. Why, I'm only going to offer this old lord half of what I intended now that I've seen it.

L: I wouldn't advise it. The ghost of the castle ...

M: Nonsense! There are no such things as ghosts. Typical! The whole country is living in the past. I just drove up in a car no bigger than a sardine box. And that on a freeway called M1 the size of a dirt track. Back home our freeways have six lanes.

L: I am also from the past and I may be part of your future, too.

M: There must be a law against it. You might be able to follow me around in Europe but not over there in the States.

L: You have seen quite a few European countries, haven't you?

M: Yes, when you have seen one, you've seen them all. You Europeans stick your noses into every hole trying to tell us normal folks what to do.

L: Sir, you have no feelings or sensitivity for people other than yourself.

M: And I'll tell you something else. You Europeans can't even get your own house in order. Call yourself a union? You all speak with different voices. Damn it! You don't even have a common language.

L: You will end in misery if you do not change your ways.

M: Who are you anyway? What is your history? If you really are a ghost as you want me to believe, you should have shaped up your own life or rather your death by now. Why don't you just disappear instead of hanging around these old buildings. Most of them should certainly be torn down.

L: (*suddenly becoming much bigger, opening her toothless mouth and cackling*) Look at the black window pane. There you can look into your future.

In the window Joe sees himself in the middle of his oilfield which is on fire; he is trapped in his Cadillac. The witch cackled again and disappeared.

 **Small talk SKILLS**

1. Tough talk versus soft talk

Beware of stereotypes! Joe Mushmellow is of course a grossly exaggerated specimen of an American small-talker. However, according to one widespread stereotype certain Americans (and Germans) tend to use tough talk. Like Joe they say directly what they mean:

I just drove ... on a freeway called M1 the size of a dirt track.
Back home our freeways have six lanes.

According to another generalisation, the educated English small-talker would express the same criticism in a more indirect way (see page 27, 88 and 134). Let's exaggerate the soft talk a bit:

I must admit that compared to your busy British motor-ways our American freeways seem somewhat oversized.

Sensitive small-talking is partly a matter of knowing certain special expressions which are gentle but don't change the basic message. So the tough talk of:

You all speak with different voices. ... You don't even have a common language.

may be transformed in their soft talk version:

I've frequently been wondering how you Europeans with your rich variety of languages manage to communicate effectively.

Let's add tough talk to our list of the deadly sins. More about this in our **Small talk plus** section.

2. Monologue versus dialogue

Did you realise that both Joe and the ghost were talking to themselves rather than talking to each other? Here are a few rules about what a dialogue really is.

Monologue	Dialogue
Ask no questions	Ask questions
Answer your own questions	Wait for others to answer
Talk for more than three minutes	Notice and respond to reactions
Fill up silences	Be comfortable with little silences
Ignore newcomers to the group	Involve newcomers

 **Small talk AWARENESS**

TASK 1: **Which of the deadly sins has Joe not committed? Tick them off**

Thou shalt not

1. bore people with too many details
2. interrupt them when they talk about their problems
3. boast of your own achievements
4. over-question people in a negative way
5. try to be better than another
6. try to seek free advice at the expense of another
7. refuse to adapt to another's mood
8. be insensitive to your partner's problems
9. evaluate or look down on the lives of others
10. be a bigot on any matter or in any meeting

FOCUS 1 : Small talk at cross-purposes

The problem with the second half of our century is that the art of small-talking seems to be disappearing. Modern literature is full of characters who are unable to small talk in a meaningful way.

Here's an excerpt from Harold Pinter's play Tea Party. It is evening. Disson (**D**), Willy (**W**) and Diana (**Di**) are in Disson's house trying to unlock common memories. Just like the Lady of the Castles and Joe Mushmallow they are talking at cross-purposes.

D: Tell me about Sunderly.

W: Sunderly?

D: Tell me about the place where you two were born. Where you played at being brother and sister.

W: We didn't have to play at brother and sister. We were brother and sister.

Di: Stop drinking.

D: Drinking? You call this drinking? This? I used to down eleven or nine pints a night! Eleven or nine pints! Every night of the stinking week! Me and the boys! The boys! And me! I'd break any man's hand for... for playing me false. That was before I became a skilled craftsman. That was before ... (*He falls silent, sits.*)

W: Sunderley was beautiful.

D: I know.

W: And now it's gone, for ever.

D: I never got there. (*He stands, goes to get a drink.*)

Di: What are you whispering about? Do you think I don't hear? Think I don't see? I've got my memories, too. Long before this.

W: Yes, Sunderley was beautiful.

D: The lake.

W: The lake.

D: The long windows.

W: From the withdrawing-room.

D: On to the terrace.

W: Music playing.

D: On the piano.

W: The summer nights. The wild swans.

D: What swans? What bloody swans?

W: The owls.

D: Negroes at the gate, under the trees.

W: No Negroes.

D: Why not?

W: We had no Negroes.

D: Why in God's name not?

W: Just one of those family quirks ...

Small talk PLUS 1 : Soften your talk

Here is a list of "softeners" that transform tough talk into soft talk. In most situations you have to combine them.

1. Use *would, could, might* to make your statement less direct.
   Money is no problem.   Money *would* be no problem.

2. Use questions to present opinions or suggestions.
   I want to meet on the 24th.   Could we meet on the 24th?

3. Use *not/n't* to allow for contradiction.
   The castle is too old.   Is*n't* the castle too old?

4. Use words like *a bit, a little, slight(ly)* to appear more flexible.
   Isn't the castle too old?   Isn't the castle *a bit* too old?

5. Use *not* with a positive word instead of a negative one.
   This hotel is dirty.   This hotel is *not very clean.*

Enough for the moment. You'll find more in chapter 14.

TASK 2: | **Say it the soft way**

Here are a few statements. Combine the above "softeners" to make these statements less direct.

1. I prefer to meet before that date.
2. Friday would be convenient.
3. Isn't that too late.
4. I need more time.
5. I'm unhappy with that suggestion.

FOCUS 2 : Intelligence Quotient versus Emotional Quotient

People like Mushmallow need not be intelligent to succeed in life. He is lucky, he is rich, oil-rich. What about the rest of us, the intelligent poor? How can we account for the fact that we, with all our intellectual abilities, are not successful in life?

In the 1940s a long-term study was conducted among 90 Harvard graduates. It showed that those with the better exams were not happier or richer at the age of forty nor did they enjoy a higher social status than those with not so brilliant academic results. A similar study was made with 450 sons of immigrants. Seven percent of men with an IQ below 90 had been unemployed for more than ten years, but so were seven percent with an IQ over 100. Intelligence is obviously not the only explanation for failure and success. For most of the century, scientists have left the powers of the heart for the poets to deal with and have worshipped the hardware of the brain and the software of the mind. However, they simply could not explain, why some good-for-nothings just seem to have a gift for doing well, or why the smartest kids in the class drive taxis or sell hamburgers. A low EQ (emotional quotient) may be the reason why many people with an IQ of 160 work for people with an IQ of 90. New brain research suggests that we have to redefine intelligence. Your emotions, not your IQ, may be the true measure of your intelligence.

Today scientists agree that IQ only accounts for about 20 percent of success in life. The rests depends on luck, your social class and on your emotional skills.

These emotional skills consist of

▶ your ability to manage failures and frustrations, anger and anxiety, worries and pessimism, pride and prejudices

▶ and your ability to manage people. Managing people is to 70 percent small talk and networking skills.

Time for a smile

Intelligence is one of the gifts that God has handed out most democratically. Everybody thinks they have got enough. *G.B. Shaw*

Small talk PLUS 2: Emotional Quotient

TASK 3: | **Test your EQ**

Unlike IQ, which is expressed in figures, EQ does not lend itself to numerical measure. Some aspects, however, can be quantified. Here are eight situations that Martin Seligman from the University of Pennsylvania has designed. Imagine how you would react and then choose the response (A or B) that comes closest to it.

1. You forget your wife's (boyfriend's/girlfriend's) birthday.
   A. I'm not good at remembering birthdays.
   B. I was preoccupied with other things.

2. You owe the library $10 for an overdue book.
   A. I was so involved in writing the report, I forgot to return the book.
   B. When I'm really involved in reading, I often forget when it's due.

3. You lose your temper with a friend.
   A. He or she is always nagging me.
   B. He or she was in a hostile mood.

4. You are penalised for returning your income-tax form late.
   A. I was lazy about getting my taxes done this year.
   B. I always put off doing my taxes.

5. You have been feeling run-down.
   A. I never get a chance to relax.
   B. I was exceptionally busy this week.

6. A friend says something that hurts your feelings.
   A. My friend was in a bad mood and took it out on me.
   B. He/she always blurts out without thinking of others.

7. You fall down a great deal while skiing.
   A. The trails were icy.
   B. Skiing is difficult.

8. You gain weight over the holidays, and you can't lose it.
   A. The diet I tried didn't work.
   B. Diets don't work in the long run.

WORD AID

grossly exaggerated	*weit übertrieben*
according to	*gemäß*
account for something	*etwas erklären*
advise	*raten, Rat geben*
art	*Kunst*
blurt out	*herausplatzen (mit)*
brain	*Gehirn*
brain research	*Hirnforschung*
cackle (v; n)	*gackern; gackerndes Lachen*
century	*Jahrhundert*
closest; come ~ to	*am nächsten kommen*
coffin	*Sarg*
commit a sin	*eine Sünde begehen*
consist of	*bestehen aus*
contradiction	*Widerspruch*
craftsman	*Handwerker*
cross-purposes; be at ~ ~	*aneinander vorbeireden*
depend on	*abhängen von*
disappear	*verschwinden*
down a pint	*eine Halbe Bier hinter die Binde kippen*
educated	*wohlerzogen; gebildet*
exaggerate	*übertreiben*
false; play someone ~	*jemanden beim Spiel betrügen*
freeway	*Autobahn (USA)*
gain weight	*zunehmen (an Gewicht)*
generalisation	*Verallgemeinerung*
gift	*Gabe, Talent*
hostile mood	*feindselige Stimmung*
hurt someone's feelings	*jemandes Gefühle verletzen*
income-tax	*Einkommensteuer*
insurance	*Versicherung*
intend	*beabsichtigen*
involve	*mit einbeziehen, beteiligen*
lane	*Spur (auf der Autobahn)*
lend oneself to	*sich eignen für*

long-term study	*langfristige Studie*
lose one's temper	*seine Beherrschung verlieren*
M1 (Motorway 1; British)	*Autobahn 1 (A1)*
measure	*Maß*
message	*Botschaft*
misfit	*Nichtangepasste(r)*
nag	*herumnörgeln*
overdue book	*überfälliges Buch*
owl	*Eule*
pane; window ~	*Fensterscheibe*
penalised; be ~	*bestraft werden*
pile of stones	*Steinhaufen*
poke one's nose into	*seine Nase in ... hineinstecken*
prejudice	*Vorurteil*
preoccupied	*beschäftigt; besorgt*
pride	*Stolz*
put off	*auf-, verschieben*
quirk	*Marotte, Eigenart*
rent	*mieten*
response	*Antwort, Reaktion*
rubbish	*Unsinn*
run-down	*erschöpft, heruntergekommen*
sensitivity	*Feinfühligkeit*
settle one's life	*sein Leben in Ordnung bringen*
silence	*Stille, Schweigen*
size	*Größe*
smack; give someone a ~ on the nose	*jemandem eins auf die Finger geben*
soften	*mildern, besänftigen*
specimen	*Exemplar*
suggestion	*Vorschlag, Anregung*
swan	*Schwan*
tough talk	*rauhe, harte Sprache*
trapped	*eingesperrt, gefangen*
underpants	*Unterhosen*
unemployed	*arbeitslos*
wing	*Flügel*
worship	*verehren*

A FAREWELL SPEECH

Chapter 14

A FAREWELL SPEECH

- **⁕ OUR STORY:** Good-bye, My Lord
- **Ⓢ Small talk SKILLS:** The NOW-Formula
- **Ⓐ Small talk AWARENESS:** Identifying small talk skills
- **✛ Small talk PLUS:** Soften your small talk
- **Ⓕ FOCUS:** Making a speech
  Advice for public speakers

Time for a smile

Beware of ghost-writers

The chairman of a large company always asked his elderly secretary to write the speeches for him. Although the speeches were normally a great success, he never congratulated her on her job. Shortly before she was due to retire, her boss asked for a speech he was going to make at a conference of computer experts.

Everything went smoothly for the first ten minutes. It was a brilliant speech full of hard facts, amusing jokes and snappy quotations that suited the occasion. When the chairman turned the third page of his manuscript he went pale. An awkward silence followed. He read in big letters: **From now on you are on your own, you old bastard.**

⊛ Good-bye, My Lord

Well, the following morning Joe Marshmallow wasn't at breakfast.

Earl of Chutsworth (**C**), von Brausewitz (**B**),
Sir Harry (**H**), John the butler (**J**)

C: Did you get a good night's sleep, von Brausewitz? I certainly did.

B: But Mushmallow obviously didn't. He shot off like a rocket this morning. Talked about seeing a witch or ghost or something.

C: A ghost you say? There is no such thing as a ghost, at least not in my castle. Ghost or no ghost, I've lost that deal. Can't say I'm sorry somehow. But if you happen to come across a decent fellow who is interested in my estate, let me know, won't you?

B: Would you also let me know in case you come across families who are looking for a decent real estate agent?[1]

C: Well, as you smart businessmen would say "You scratch my back and I'll scratch yours."

B: We'll keep in touch.

So a couple of weeks passed and Brausy was invited to the farewell party of one of his customers. He had arranged the sale of Bloomsbury Mansion, the twenty-five room family home of Sir Harry Bloomsbury OBE. Sir Harry throws a farewell party for his staff.

H: Ladies and Gentlemen, much as it pains me to say it, this will be my last speech in front of the staff of this old home. Circumstances have obliged me to put this house up for sale and to conclude a contract which passes the property into new ownership. The joyful part of the transaction is that the human element, yourselves, will remain in place here. Only my person and my family will leave. This is a sorrow for us and for our family as Bloomsbury has been our ancestral home for two hundred years. On the other hand, as far as we are informed the new master of Bloomsbury will be a fair man and you may look forward to him. As for yourselves I would like to thank you heartily for your efforts and your patience. Thank you.

J: (*with a tray*) Excuse me, you look as if you could do with a drink, sir. This is all very heart-breaking, isn't it?[2]

B: Yes indeed. My God, what a speech!

J: You must be Mr Brausewitz, I presume. You negotiated the business, I heard?

B: Yes, and I don't feel good about it. Eh, how long have you worked here, John?

J: Thirty years, sir. It was a great time.

B: So you've felt at home and well-treated here at the estate?[3]

J: Of course, there were problems now and again, but then life's full of problems, isn't it? This ceremony is very touching, sir, don't you find?[4]

B: Yes, it is. Sir Harry made a beautiful speech, didn't he? Short and to the point.

J: And in a way the whole ceremony is beautiful but at the same time very depressing. Sorry, I've got to go now. I have to say a few words of gratitude. See you later.

J: (*fade-in*) ... And so I think I'm speaking on behalf of all of us when I say to Sir Harry Bloomsbury thank-you for the many interesting years. We wish you the best for the future. And now a toast to Sir Harry and his family. Sir Harry, all the best, sir.

H: Well, I'm overcome. Thank you very much. (*fade-out*)
(*fade-in*) ... and it's all very difficult today. I'd never expected the staff to react with so much feeling.

B: They're obviously very fond of you, sir.[3]

H: I really don't know what to say.

B: Socialists![4]

H: I beg your pardon?

B: Socialists! Once they get in there's a problem for all of us with property or business. They tend to milk the private sector dry.

H: Well, I agree with you there. That reminds me ... (*fade-out*)

Time for a smile

The newly appointed chairman of a group of companies was nervously studying the notes for his speech when the toastmaster walked up to him and asked: "Are you ready to speak, sir? Or shall we allow them to enjoy themselves a little longer?"

Small talk SKILLS : The NOW-Formula

Speech and conversation have one thing in common: a good way to open them is to comment on the situation or the occasion. Be aware of the "here and now" and put it into words. It is one way to move to common ground. The NOW-Formula offers you three ways of doing it.

> **N**otice your neighbour
> **O**bserve the occasion
> **W**atch out for things and express your admiration

1. Notice other people

"Noticing statements" are excellent small talk openers because they show you are aware of the other person. They show that you are interested.

> You look so healthy and tanned. Did you spend the holidays in the mountains?
> I noticed that you really enjoyed giving that presentation. You seem to have a lot of experience talking in front of groups.

The conversation becomes more personal and it encourages the other person to notice something about you.

2. Observe the occasion

One way to begin a speech or a conversation is to make remarks about the occasion, the cause of your being together. If you are at a conference or a business meeting you might ask:

> What looks interesting to you on the agenda?
> What do you think is the most important issue on the agenda?
> What do you hope to get out of this?

Thus you quickly move on to asking for opinions and evaluations.

3. Watch out for things you can see hear or smell

Another way to begin is to comment on what you have just heard, what you can see or smell. A basket of flowers could lead to a dozen different topics. In an office, look for posters, pictures or awards on the wall, or objects on the desk. Comment on what you see:

What a beautiful Japanese statue you've got there.
Is there a story behind it?

Don't ask questions like these!

Where did you get it?
How much did you pay for it?

People might think you want to go right out and buy one just like it.

4. The psychoanalyst's technique

A session with a psychoanalyst only seems to be a dialogue. In reality it is a monologue. He listens to you and to keep you unlocking your memories he just feeds back your own ideas in other words.

Patient: It was a humiliating experience for me ... (silence) ...
Doctor: So, it made you feel bad, didn't it?

He plays the ball back into your court without adding a new idea or asking a new question. Experienced small-talkers use this technique either to make you talk or when they don't know exactly how to respond but want to keep the ball rolling.

Time for a smile

Beware of ghost-writers
Did you hear about the elderly company chairman who, one day, said to his personal assistant "Dobson, I'll need a twenty-minute speech, and make it light and humorous. I'm speaking at a meeting of the National Golf Club Association."
The following day the chairman stormed in. "Dobson," he shouted, "that was the lousiest speech you ever wrote for me – and what was more, it lasted for an hour."
"Ah," said the assistant, "I wonder if that might have anything to do with the fact that I gave you two carbon copies."

A Small talk AWARENESS

We've numbered some lines in the dialogue. Can you identify the small talk skills?

TASK 1: **Then put the numbers next to the technique.**

Noticing statement to start a conversation
The "springboard technique". Why is it used here?
The psychoanalyst's technique
Trying to find a network partner

Small talk PLUS : Soften your small talk (2)

Here is another list of "softeners" that change tough talk into soft talk. In most situations you have to use them in combination with those "softeners" in chapter 13.

1. Prepare the listener for a negative message (see list below)
   Tom, our financial situation   *Actually*, Tom, our financial
   is disastrous.   situation *isn't too bright*.

2. Add *I'm afraid* for a negative response.
   I can't meet you this week.   *I'm afraid I wouldn't* be able to meet
                                  you this week.

3. Use a comparative to soften your message
   An early delivery will be helpful   An *earlier* delivery *would* be more
                                      helpful.

4. The continuous form (Verlaufsform) makes statements flexible.
   I tried to ring you yesterday.   I was trying to ring you yesterday.

How to prepare people for a negative message

Actually,	With respect,	As a matter of fact,
Well,	To be honest,	To put it bluntly,
Frankly,	In fact,	In those circumstances,

TASK 2: **Say it the soft way**

Here are a few statements. Use these "softeners" together with those in chapter 13 to make these statements less direct.

1. I wondered if you'd come to a decision yet.
2. It's a good idea to make an early decision.
3. Research is needed before we make a decision.
4. That's an impractical decision.
5. I don't like that idea at all.

 **FOCUS 1 : Making a speech**

One of the main obstacles to success is fear of failure. Very often speakers just put off preparing their speeches until the last moment, and that's a recipe for disaster. So begin by putting your energy into preparing a speech that will please your audience and give you peace of mind.

Knowing how to tell a humorous story, make a toast or a speech belongs to the small talk skills of the businessman. For all but the most extrovert, an invitation to make a speech is something to be dreaded. But it needn't be, particularly if you are in business. As a businessman you have some advantages when it comes to making public speeches.

▶ If you are used to making presentations you won't have difficulties making a short speech.
▶ As a business person you have a lot to talk about. Who doesn't have a funny story to tell about their subordinates, colleagues or bosses? And who hasn't experienced the pleasures and problems of office life?
▶ When you stand up to give a speech about the world of business, you can be sure that most of the people in your audience will be able to identify with you.

As a businessman you are versed in the art of persuasion; you know how to assess customers, weigh up situations and respond appropriately. All these skills are directly applicable when it comes to making a public speech. We'll give you a few hints on how to get it right.

FOCUS 2 : Advice for public speakers

Know your audience

1. Contact the organiser of the event and find out if there's anything special or interesting about the occasion.
2. Collect all information you can get about the participants.
3. Find out what kind of mood the audience will be in and what will please them in that mood.

Be aware of the occasion

1. Strike the tone of the occasion. A five-minute speech at a lunchtime engagement may be sharp and witty – particularly if everyone has to go back to work afterwards.
2. A toast should create a sense of community so that everybody is able to join you in the toast. It should last two to three minutes.
3. An after-dinner speech at the end of dining and wining can be more robust in tone. Don't talk for more than five to ten minutes.

Avoid typical mistakes

1. Don't read your speech. Plan and rehearse it days before.
2. Take your time. Don't start your speech until everyone is ready and listening.
3. Don't talk like a schoolmaster. This is not the occasion to speak about your convictions and principles.
4. Don't try to revamp an old speech or use old material.
5. Don't change your speech at the last minute. Neither improvise any part of your speech nor extend it.

Humorous speech openers

1. After the host has introduced you with a few flattering remarks you could say:
   After such a warm reception I can hardly wait to hear myself speak.
2. If you are nervous about making a speech, start with a modest apology.
   Before I begin my speech I'd like to warn you that I'm suffering from a severe handicap – I'm sober.
   I am here to speak to you, you are here to listen to me. If you finish first, please let me know.

3. If your talk is going to be very short, prepare your audience for it:
A bore is a person with nothing to say who insists on saying it.
The best speeches are like a well-kept lawn: short and neat.

WORD AID

applicable	*anwendbar, übertragbar*
appoint someone	*jemanden ernennen*
appropriate(ly)	*angemessen*
audience	*Publikum*
behalf; on ~ of	*im Namen von*
bluntly; put it ~	*ungeschminkt; es ~ sagen*
carbon copy	*Durchschlag*
circumstance	*Umstand*
comparative	*Steigerung*
crucial moment	*entscheidender Augenblick*
deal	*Geschäft, Handel*
decent	*anständig*
decision	*Entscheidung*
disastrous	*katastrophal*
dread	*fürchten*
effort	*Mühe, Anstrengung*
encourage	*ermutigen*
evaluation	*Bewertung, Einschätzung*
failure	*Misserfolg*
farewell	*Abschiedsfeier*
flattering remarks	*Schmeicheleien*
heartily	*herzlich*
hint	*Hinweis, Fingerzeig*
humiliating	*demütigend*
insist on	*bestehen auf*
lawn	*Rasen*
mood	*Stimmung*
negotiate	*ver-, aushandeln*
obviously	*offensichtlich*
obstacle	*Hindernis*

occasion	*Anlass, Gelegenheit*
overcome	*überwältigen*
participant	*Teilnehmer*
presume	*annehmen, vermuten*
reception	*Empfang*
recipe	*Kochrezept*
recognition	*Anerkennung*
rehearse	*proben*
remain	*bleiben*
response	*Antwort, Reaktion*
revamp	*aufmöbeln*
rocket	*Rakete*
sale	*Verkauf*
scratch	*kratzen*
senior executive	*leitender Angestellter*
session	*Sitzung*
shareholder	*Aktionär*
sleepwalk	*schlafwandeln*
sober	*nüchtern*
sorrow	*Kummer*
staff	*Personal*
subordinate	*Untergebener*
tanned	*sonnengebräunt*
touching	*rührend*
treat	*behandeln*
used to	*gewöhnt an*
versed in	*versiert in*
witch	*Hexe*

Time for a smile

"Why did you walk out in the middle of my speech?" demanded the company chairman of one of his senior executives. "It was an important meeting of shareholders and you chose the most crucial moment to walk out when I had been speaking for only forty minutes."
"I'm sorry, sir," replied the senior executive, "but it was nothing personal. I was just sleepwalking."

CONGRATULATIONS AT THE COMPANY

Chapter 15

CONGRATULATIONS AT THE COMPANY

✳	**OUR STORY:**	As time goes by
⟳	**Small talk SKILLS:**	The Five-Finger Formula for amateur speakers
		The sign of sparkle
Ⓐ	**Small talk AWARENESS:**	Identifying small talk skills
✛	**Small talk PLUS:**	Speech functions
Ⓕ	**FOCUS:**	The Fifth E – Expand your network

Time for a smile

How to make an exit

The inventor Thomas Alva Edison had little time for formal dinners. Once, finding himself surrounded by people with whom he had nothing in common, he wanted to escape as soon as possible. But as he was inching towards the door, he was approached by his hostess, who said "I'm so pleased that you could come, Mr Edison. Tell me what are you working on now?" – "My exit," replied the inventor.

Groucho Marx was leaving a particularly boring party. At the door he said to the hostess "I've had a wonderful evening – but this wasn't it."

✳ As time goes by

Meanwhile back at the office in York things are going on as usual. It is lunch-time and there is an official celebration of 25 years of service for Tim Jones from the accounts department. At the King's Head:

Roger Devenshire (**R**), von Brausewitz (**B**), Tim Jones (**T**)

R: And so we're gathered together, if I might steal a phrase from the Bible, to congratulate Tim on his 25th year of pleasure in our little enterprise. As we look back over the years we see that everything was, perhaps, not as rosy as it could have been. There were ups and downs as there are in every walk of life. Tim, you have certainly seen many changes around here. I remember our first year together, our founding year. I think we were only five people at that time. Now we are 29. You can't know everybody nowadays. Our latest member joined us just three months ago. You may not all know Fritz von Brausewitz. Stand up and be seen, Fritz. Thank you. Well, Gentlemen I'd like to say a hearty thankyou to Tim for the last 25 years and here's to the next 25. To you, Tim.[1] Thank you. (*Clinking of two glasses*)

Others: Here, here. Speech!

T: Well everybody, before I begin my speech I'd like to warn you that I'm suffering from a severe handicap: I'm still sober. And you all know that in that state I'm not particularly good with words. Being an accountant I'm more into figures. I wasn't hired to make speeches. Roger hired me to explain to the tax people that he didn't make the money he did … (*fade out*)

(*fade in*) … and so I'd just like to say thank you all very much and I hope I'll be around a lot longer. Please all relax now and enjoy the champagne or just yourselves. Here's to the future of our company.[1]

Others: Great. Yeah!!! (*Sound of pouring champagne*)

(*Von Brausewitz talking to Tim*)

B: We only met briefly at the last office party. I'm Fritz.

T: Hi. You're the newest and I'm the oldest.[2]

B: I mean 25 years is a long stretch.[3] Have you got any tips for me in that respect?[4]

T: You're right, it's a long sentence. And I couldn't have made it if I'd taken the job too seriously.

B: So you took your work in a relaxed way?[4] That's quite difficult.

T: My priority was always my spare time. I'm a passionate hiker.

B: Are you indeed?[5] So am I. I try to walk every weekend. Where do you walk?

T: Mostly in the Peak District or the Pennines. Listen I can ... (*fade out*)

Small talk SKILLS

1. The Five-Finger Formula for amateur speakers

The problem with informal speeches is that we are not supposed to read them, and if we give them without a manuscript we are nervous and risk getting stuck in the middle of the speech. The Five-Finger Formula is an easy aid-memoire. A speech should have three parts:

a beginning, a middle and an end.

Each part should consist of three messages. And your five fingers help you not to forget any of them. Move each finger three times as you are spinning your yarn.

Thumb reminds you to tell them	1. who you are, 2. why you are here and 3. what you are going to talk about "with great pleasure" (Roger referred to the occasion.)
Forefinger reminds you of	the first part of the middle of your talk. Begin with your first argument or example. (Roger talked about the past.)
Middle finger reminds you of	your second argument or example. (Roger referred to the present situation.)
Ring finger reminds you of	your third argument or example. (Roger looked to the future.)
Little finger reminds you	to round off: tell them what you've told them, draw a conclusion and thank them for their attention. (Roger proposed a toast.)

2. The sign of sparkle (electric moment)

Once I was interviewing trainees at my Weinheim company. They were applying for placements abroad at our subsidiaries in foreign countries. I came across one candidate who showed no interest in anything. The conversation was dragging along painfully for both of us, interrupted by long moments of awkward silence. Then I asked my last standard question: "What do you do in your spare time?" – "I breed bonsai", he replied. "Tell me more", I replied and a transformation took place – he became animated, leant forward, and spoke like a real enthusiast non-stop for ten minutes.

His English was ungrammatical, his accent hard to follow, but he got his message across to me; he was a different person. We sent him to one of our plantations in Latin America.

Why am I telling you this story? Well, it illustrates what we call "the sign of sparkle". You will know it when you hit upon a theme that makes your partner's eyes glow with interest or even enthusiasm. It signals the beginning of enjoyable small talk.

Experienced small-talkers collect information about their business partners' hobbies or fields of interests to find a suitable present and to spark off a conversation with them when the right moment has come. By the way, did you notice the sign of sparkle in our story?

A Small talk AWARENESS

TASK 1: Identifying small talk skills

You already know the name of the game. So put the right number next to the small talk skill.

Small talk skill	no
The psychoanalyst's technique	
The sign of the sparkle	
Proposing a toast	
Small talk with a purpose	
Finding common ground	

Small talk PLUS : Speech functions

TASK 2: **Complete the speech functions**

reason		pleasure		gathering
	propose		occasion	
chance		nutshell		attention

The reason for our .... is ...

The .... of today's meeting is ...

The .... for our coming together is to ...

I'm glad to have the .... to speak to you about ...

Nothing gives me greater ....

I've been asked to .... a toast to ...

To put it in a ....: All's well that ends well.

Thank you for your attention, ladies and gentlemen.

TASK 3: **Rearrange the speech**

Use the finger formula and rearrange this speech by numbering the five parts.

Little did I think when I first saw Anne torturing the cat at the age of five that she would one day become the manager of a successful company and a loving wife.

I've been asked to propose a toast the health of Ron and Anne. Nothing gives me greater pleasure.

I'm not going to say anything about Ron because he has the stature of a Sumo ringer and we all know his temper.

So I will conclude by raising my glass to the health of the young couple. Let's wish them all the best for a successful first marriage.

I've often used Sydney Smith's definition: "Marriage resembles a pair of shears so joined that they cannot be separated, often moving in opposite directions, yet always punishing anyone who comes between them."

 **FOCUS : The fifth E – Expand your network**

Make your friends and acquaintances your first network partners. Start with people you know already: school friends, former colleagues, persons that have studied with you. With most of them you are still on first-name terms. If you know just 50 persons on a first-name basis, and if each of them knows another 50 people you have already 2,500 friends of friends. Warm up cold contacts and turn them into network partners. By the way, most small talk techniques work on the phone as well as in writing.

▶ Phone them up to tell them that you have met a mutual acquaintance.
▶ Send them Christmas cards and cards from your holiday.
▶ Phone them up on their birthdays.
▶ Phone them up when you read about them in the press.
▶ Send them articles which you feel would be of interest to them.
▶ Find out if you have mutual acquaintances, common interests and connections: hobbies, sports, social interests, plans for trips or holidays. Make an appointment or invite them out.
▶ Talk about the old days and what has become of friends you have lost sight of.

Get your "shopping list" ready when you meet them. You shouldn't expect any specific favour. However, when they ask you about your job you may mention what kind of information you have been looking for.

Where to look for new network partners

You find them in / at / on a ...		
conference	training course	party
congress	seminar	sports club
exhibition	hotel	school meeting
pub	church	funeral
waiting room	train	plane

How to contact potential network partners

▶ Tell the receptionist or the barman that you would like to meet certain people: architects, manufacturers or scientists etc. For a small tip they will give you a hint or even establish the contact.

▶ Ask your children if they know what the parents of their friends and schoolmates do for a living. There are lots of opportunities to establish a relationship with their parents.

▶ Let your customers and suppliers know what you are interested in and where you would like to expand your network. Offer them the same service.

▶ Keep in touch with former colleagues who now work for other companies and exchange useful information.

▶ Members of your political party, students organisation or sports club are easy to approach. After a tennis match or a glass of beer it is easy to talk business.

▶ If you know your host well, you could ask him to introduce you to people you want to meet. Your network partners will do that without being asked.

Time for a smile

During a dinner party a hostess sitting at the opposite end of the table to a great friend scribbled a note to her and asked the butler to deliver it discreetly. Unfortunately the lady couldn't read without her glasses. So she asked the man seated on her left to help her out.

"Please be a dear," he read "and try to liven up the man on your left. He's a terrible bore, but see if you can talk to him."

WORD AID AID

accounts department	*Buchhaltung*
aid-memoire	*Gedächtnisstütze*
animated	*lebhaft*
approach	*ansprechen*
awkward silence	*peinliche Stille*
briefly	*kurz*
celebration	*Feier*
conclude by saying	*mit den Worten enden*
conclusion	*Schlussfolgerung*
dear; be a ~	*sei so lieb*
drag along	*sich dahinziehen*
enthusiasm	*Begeisterung*
exit	*Abgang; Ausgang*
founding year	*Gründungsjahr*
gather	*sich versammeln*
inch towards	*sich langsam zubewegen auf*
liven up	*aufheitern, aufmuntern*
mutual acquaintance	*gemeinsame Bekannte(r)*
particularly	*besonders*
placement	*Praktikum*
punish	*strafen*
refer to	*verweisen auf*
respect; in this ~	*diesbezüglich*
scribble	*kritzeln*
shears; a pair of ~	*Gartenschere*
sober	*nüchtern*
spare time	*Freizeit*
sparkle	*Glanz, Funkeln*
suffer from	*leiden an / unter*
supplier	*Lieferant*
supposed; be ~ to do	*etwas tun sollen*
surround	*umgeben*
torture	*quälen*
ups and downs	*Höhen und Tiefen*
walk; in every ~ of life	*auf allen Lebenswegen*
yarn; spin one's ~	*sein Garn spinnen*

OUR STORY: The status meeting
Small talk SKILLS: To joke or not to joke ...
Small talk PLUS: How to tell a story or a joke
FOCUS: From small talk to business

Time for a smile

How to tell a joke

As the years rolled by, the prisoners in the top security prison soon exhausted their supply of jokes. In fact so familiar had the jokes become that they had taken to numbering them to save them the trouble of telling the stories. They just said the numbers.

One day, desperate for amusement, one of them said he wanted to tell a joke. "OK, let's hear it," said his cell-mates.

"26."

Not a laugh, not even a smile. "I'll try another one then: 16." Still no response. "It's a good joke, that number 16," said one of the prisoners, "but, like they say, it's the way you tell them, you know."

147

⊛ The status meeting

Brausy wasn't feeling too good about his work. He often dreamed of people in misery forced to sell everything. "There but for the grace of God go I," he thought. He was going to have what he expected to be a difficult meeting on the next day. During the night the Lady of the castles came in a dream: "Now is the time," she whispered. "What the devil does she mean by that?" he wondered.

> Conference room at Castles and Titles Incorporated, one late Friday evening. Roger Devenshire (**R**), Andrew Dobson (**A**), Tim Jones (**T**), von Brausewitz (**B**)

T: I heard you've been getting a bit of walking in at the weekends. A bit of relaxation is necessary, isn't it?

B: It really is. I must say I've not been feeling too good recently, with the work I mean.

T: Your heart's not in it. I can sense that. And I don't think today's meeting will help the situation much, either.

B: Right. I don't have a good feeling about it, either.
(noise of people talking, Roger banging on the table)

R: Right, gentlemen. I'd like to declare this meeting open. Today you have no agenda in front of you and no pre-meeting hand-outs although I think some of you can guess what it's all about. I'll come to the point. Fritz, we seem to be having some problems, don't we? Tim, would you like to give us a short summary?

T: Well, what Roger is referring to is our failure to conclude contracts with a couple of major potential customers.

R: Yes, we've missed quite a lot of turnover that quite honestly we'd reckoned with. I mean the contract with the Earl of Chutsworth and Joe Mushmallow and the Gilmore Estate. We'd like your comments, Fritz.

B: Well, first of all we did sign a contract with Gilmore, true only for part of the estate, but ...

A: *(interrupting)* And what was the reason for the whole project not going through?

B: Well, the owner didn't have the heart to sell everything.

R: My information is that you offered an alternative partial solution. Why was that?

B: (*speaking more slowly and looking Roger squarely in the eyes*) I felt this was the better advice for the customer. I did what I considered to be fair.

R: Fair for him, but not for us.

T: I say, Roger, Fritz was only doing what he thought best in the given situation.

R: Yes, I'm sure he was. But Fritz, we'd like to hear what happened at Chutsworth.

B: It seems that Mushmallow saw a ghost that night and ran away the following morning. I couldn't change the situation and ...

R: (*interrupting*) Are you seriously expecting us to believe that Joe Mushmellow was frightened away by a ghost? You must be joking!

B: According to those who study psychic phenomena, Britain has the highest density of ghosts in the world.

T: Yes, but only in the world of legends, fairy tales ... and jokes, of course. By the way, do you know the joke about the ghost that entered a bar and ordered a whisky? ... The barman said: "Sorry – no spirits served here."

A: You've told that one before.

T: Here's another. What do you call a female ghost who serves drinks and food on an aeroplane? ... An air ghostess.

B: (*interrupting*) Very funny! Whatever you may say, I have had the same or a similar experience to Joe Mushmallow's myself. Several times.

A: My God we're building our business on visions and ghosts. (*he makes "tutting" noises*)

R: Fritz, are you sure you're not letting personal feelings get the better of you?

B: Maybe I am letting my feelings get the better of me, but I don't like the direction the business is taking. And I saw the ghost. If you don't believe me then I will take the consequences.

R: Surely you must see that all this talk of spirits is crazy? I don't believe in ghosts and I don't think they believe in me either ... (*At that moment the lights flickered, a gust of wind blew through the window and all the papers drifted off the conference table. Roger went pale.*)

B: Gentlemen, I have made up my mind. I hereby offer my resignation. You will receive it tomorrow in writing. Good-day.

 **Small talk SKILLS : To joke or not to joke**

1. When to joke

Psychologists have proved that jokes are healthy because laughter helps people to relax.

- Jokes create atmosphere, they bring a bit of sunshine into a gloomy day.
- You can use them as ice-breakers in meetings and negotiations, if they fit the occasion.
- If something goes wrong during a presentation a witty quotation can save the day.
- If you are nervous about making a speech, a modest joke will help you to overcome your nervousness.

2. When not to joke

Jokes can go badly wrong because they are a matter of tact and taste. If they fall flat or if somebody feels offended everyone will be embarrassed and serious small-talkers will leave the group.

Jokes have a tendency to be used when people can't think of anything else to talk about. Some people feel encouraged to tell a better joke. This is often the beginning of a "can-you-top-this"? competition and the end of enjoyable small talk.

3. The alternative – anecdotes and stories

Dry facts will go down better if you wrap them up in a story. And if you are a good story-teller, you will be remembered together with your story. A humorous story can bridge the gap when the guest speaker does not arrive on time because his train has been delayed. Public speakers and managers who want to promote team spirit, productivity or customer service prefer amusing stories or anecdotes to jokes.

4. The power of humorous stories and anecdotes

All the great leaders in history from Jesus to Ghandi knew about the power of storytelling.

- Stories are more flexible in so far as it is easier to adapt them to a situation.
- They arouse attention and curiosity.
- They are non-offensive.
- They engage the imagination.
- They make complex things understandable.
- They make ideas more memorable.
- They illustrate your argument.
- They permit new associations.
- They invite action.

Small talk PLUS

1. How to tell a story

The beginning: Describe the situation using as few words as possible.
The middle: There should be a problem, a crisis, an obstacle or a climax.
Dramatise your story, use direct speech.
The ending: It is the solution, a moral or an evaluation.
Use body language.
Practise with a tape recorder.

2. How to tell a joke

Here are some speech functions that might help you to announce jokes and to comment on jokes.

Introducing a good joke
Do you know the one about ...?
Do you know the latest joke about ...?
Have you heard the latest joke ?
Did you hear about ...?
Now here's a funny thing ...

Interrupting someone with a joke

How interesting! That reminds me of a joke: ...
That reminds me of the one about ...
That was a good one! May I just tell you one more about ...?

3. Encouraging someone to tell the joke

Tell it!
Let's hear it!

4. Showing that you have (not) understood the joke

The penny's dropped.
That's a good one.
I don't get it.
I don't get that one.
Where's the joke?

5. Silencing the storyteller

What's so funny about that?
You've told that one before.
We've heard that one before.
We know that one already.
That's so old.

Time for a smile

Henry Ford once set sail for Europe in a Peace Ship accompanied by other famous pacifists. Their intention was to bring World War I to an end by appealing to the various heads of state. Unfortunately the plan did not work and the ship became known as the Ship of Fools. Ford, however did not regret his trip. "I didn't get much peace," he said, "but I learned that Russia is going to be a great market for tractors."

(F) FOCUS : From small talk to business

1. Be visible – show yourself to good effect

Small talk skills are helpful in creating business opportunities. However, it is no good going on small-talking to people while you wait for your skills to be discovered. You might be playing on the wrong stage with the wrong audience in front of you. Choose the right stage and step forward into the limelight. If you have a good product, you market it; if you want your skills to be appreciated, you have to self-market your personality. "Eighty percent of success is showing up" says Woody Allen. We recommend two stages to build your visibility:

Be read in business magazines
▶ Send letters to the letters pages
▶ Offer book reviews
▶ Write articles
▶ Send a free copy of a magazine to which you have contributed to all network partners and decision-makers

Be noticed at meetings, conferences and congresses
▶ Say your name
▶ Ask a question
▶ Make a contribution
▶ Score a point
▶ Make contacts during coffee breaks

Remember, it's not so important what you know as who you know. Yet you must have something to give to them in order to get something from them. Networking is not manipulating people, but an honest exchange by which all network partners profit.

2. Prick up your ears

A group of students in the Mannheim area collected all the information that their fellow students spend hours searching for on the Internet. They then put it on a CD-ROM. It was a hit and resulted in a company. When listening to people you can often learn about problems with products. Solving these problems can be a good source of new business ideas.

Collect information	Exploit information
What do people complain about?	There is a better service / product you could offer.
What are the people's needs that haven't yet been met?	There are new products or services to discover.
Who is the lawyer in town who specialises in cases your company has to deal with?	You might need his services one day. Try to get his phone number.
Who might be useful for my business?	Offer free advice, services or resources. Seek a long-term relationship.

WORD AID

agenda	*Tagesordnung*
anxious; be ~ to do something	*begierig sein, etwas zu tun*
appeal to someone	*jemanden ersuchen*
appreciate	*würdigen, schätzen*
bridge the gap	*die Kluft überwinden*
climax	*Höhepunkt*
conclude by saying	*abschließend sagen*
conclude contracts	*Verträge abschließen*
contribute to	*beitragen zu*
decision-maker	*Entscheidungsträger*
delayed	*verspätet*
density	*Dichte*
desperate	*verzweifelt*
evaluation	*Bewertung*
fairy tale	*Märchen*
fall flat	*hier: daneben / in die Hose gehen*
familiar	*vertraut*
fool	*Narr*
grace	*Gnade*
guess	*raten*

ignorant	*ungebildet*
limelight	*Rampenlicht*
look squarely in the eyes	*direkt in die Augen schauen*
make up one's mind	*sich entschließen*
meet a need	*ein Bedürfnis befriedigen*
non-offensive	*nicht anstößig*
partial solution	*Teillösung*
permit	*erlauben*
point; come to the ~	*zur Sache kommen*
quotation	*Zitat*
recently	*kürzlich*
refer to	*sich beziehen, verweisen auf*
regret	*bedauern*
response	*Reaktion*
score a point	*hier: eine schlaue Bemerkung machen*
services	*Dienstleistungen*
show up	*sich zeigen*
similar	*ähnlich, gleich*
spirits	*Alkohol; Geister*
supply	*Vorrat*
top; can you ~ that?	*kannst du das überbieten?*
turnover	*Umsatz*
visible	*sichtbar*
well-meaning	*wohlmeinend, gutmütig*
wrap up	*verpacken, einwickeln*

Time for a smile

A certain literary society had advertised a talk on the poet Keats and almost at the last moment had asked the mayor, a well-meaning but ignorant man, to take the chair and introduce the guest speaker. After a few remarks on the occasion he concluded by saying: "Now I'm sure you're all as anxious as I am for the speaker to begin and let us know just exactly what Keats are."

From castle-seller to castle-dweller

Brausy left Castles and Titles Incorporated. He set up business as a consultant. The name of his company was AAA, Aid to the Ailing Aristocrat. One evening he was sitting in front of a log fire in Scotland at Gilmore Estate with his fiancée, Emily. They were drinking a dram or two of the best malt whisky.

Midnight at Gilmore Estate, Scotland: Brausy (**B**), Emily (**E**),
The Lady of the Castle (**L**)

(*Suddenly, out of the corner of his eye Brausy noticed the strange beautiful White Lady again.*)

B: Hello, I understood your message. I resigned from my company. I couldn't accept the work anymore.

L: I knew you wouldn't be able to. As I promised, when there is misery I will come to you and will help you …

E: Fritz, who are you talking to? Are you okay?

B: Emily, my dear, you wouldn't believe me if I told you.

E: Try me!

B: Well, a few months ago … (*fade out*)

Several hundred miles away in the King's Head Roger (**R**) and Andrew (**A**)

R: I heard some news about Fritz the other day. Somehow I was damn sorry to lose him.

A: Yes, he had something about him.

R: Well, whatever it is he is one of the most successful consultants in the whole country. He seems to know just where to be at exactly the right time. It's eerie.

A: Yes, maybe there are ghosts after all.

R: Nonsense! There are no such things as ghosts.

FOCUS : Exceed expectations

If, in the course of small talk, someone has done you a favour or if you have offered someone a service, surprise them by exceeding their expectations. You might win your first network partner. Here are a few suggestions.

If people have done you a favour

▶ thank them in front of others for their efforts in helping you
▶ let them know if you have used one of their ideas for your work
▶ do it by phone or in writing

If you have offered them a service, surprise them by going the extra hundred metres if not a kilometre:

▶ keep your promises to the letter
▶ beat the deadline
▶ offer a better price than expected
▶ produce better quality than expected
▶ add something small

The Lady of the Castle has certainly more than kept her part of the bargain.

Time for a smile

What it means to exceed expectations
An ageing millionairess was very happy with her handsome young golf trainer who dramatically improved her technique.
"Young man," she exclaimed, "I insist on making you a present to show you my gratitude." – "Well, if you insist," the professional replied, "you can buy me some golf clubs."
The next week he received a telex: "Have bought you Wentworth and Sunningdale, but St. Andrews refused to sell."

WORD AID AID

ailing aristocrats	*Not leidende Adlige*
beat the deadline	*den Termin unterschreiten*
dram	*Tröpfchen, Schluck*
dweller	*Bewohner*
eerie	*unheimlich, gespenstisch*
effort	*Mühe, Anstrengung*
exceed	*übertreffen*
golf club	*1. Golfschläger; 2. Golfclub*
gratitude	*Dankbarkeit*
handsome	*gut aussehend*
improve	*verbessern*
log fire	*Holzfeuer*
millionairess	*Millionärin*
resign	*aufgeben, zurücktreten*
surprise	*überraschen*

SMALL TALK AROUND THE WORLD

The small-talkers guide to ten countries

1. Pride and prejudice

Beware of stereotyping. Most people are proud of their country and think that it is the best. They are convinced that their way of life, their literature, their cuisine is superior to those of the rest of the world. It is not easy to understand another culture and it is sometimes painful to adapt to it. Often we don't have enough time to discover and appreciate the ways of other nations. That is why we are critical of their food, manners and politics.

Criticism without understanding leads to ethnic stereotypes. When we stereotype a nation and its people we

- put them into categories
- attach labels
- become subjective
- forget that we are dealing with individuals
- reinforce our own prejudices.

Stereotyping is a barrier to mutual understanding because

- barriers grow up subconsciously and affect our attitude
- it creates mistrust and hostility
- people have no chance to prove that stereotypes are wrong
- prejudices spread quickly, they are contagious.

Discover the country and keep an open mind. Form an opinion of your own.

- Don't listen to friends who have had negative experiences in a foreign country. They might have been unable to adapt.
- Don't make comparisons with how things are done at home. It will only increase your frustration.
- Don't spend all your time in offices and hotels. Get out, make contacts and discover the country.
- Don't expect to be liked.

Read the following pages with a critical mind. We have mixed reality with irony. Discover the stereotypes.

2. SMALL TALK in England

Georges Mikes gives a good example that shows the difference between small talk on the Continent and small talk in England. A continental gentleman seeing a nice picture may remark:
"This view reminds me of Utrecht, where the War of Spanish Succession was signed on the 11th April, 1713. The river there, however, recalls the Guadalquivir which rises in the Sierra de Cazorla and flows into the Atlantic Ocean and is 650 kilometres long. Oh, rivers ... What did Pascal say about them? "Les rivières sont les chemins qui marchent."
An Englishman would remain silent for some time and think about how he could put his feelings into words and then say "It's pretty, isn't it?" In England it is bad manners to be clever. The educated Englishman is modest and simple.

While the American businessman is straightforward and says what he thinks, his British colleague is a good listener and keeps back his position as long as possible. As Heinrich Heine once said: "Silence can be defined as a conversation with an Englishman." He rarely disagrees openly with your proposals. He might say to a salesman: "I quite like this little device" only to go on with, "however, I'm not sure that it is of any use to my family."

Mind your manners

- ▶ Formal greetings and handshaking are customary.
- ▶ A reserved manner is expected.
- ▶ Business cards are exchanged as a matter of courtesy.
- ▶ Avoid personal questions. Neutral topics of opening conversation are more acceptable than exchanging personal information at the first meeting.
- ▶ Religion and politics are best avoided at the beginning.
- ▶ They don't use hand gestures to emphasise points and are critical of those who do.
- ▶ They won't complain when things go wrong; they will however moan and tell other people when they get home. So provide an opportunity for them to say how they feel and if anything is or was not to their liking.

3. SMALL TALK in the USA

"They don't stand on ceremony. They make no distinction about a man's background, his parentage, his education. They say what they mean, and there is a vivid muscularity about the way they say it ... They are always the first to put their hands in their pockets. They press you to visit them in their own home the moment they meet you, and they are irrepressibly good-humoured, ambitious and brimming with self-confidence in any company. Apart from that I've got nothing against them."
Tom Stoppard, Dirty Linen, 1976

Mind your manners

- They are quickly on first-name terms with you.
- Don't insist on titles.
- Small talk is important especially if it is about their trip to Europe.
- A friendly, firm handshake with good eye contact is important.
- Smiling into the eyes is very important.
- Use positive, animated helpful language. ("No problem! I'll do that right away!")
- When they ask you "How do you like the USA?" they don't expect you to give a frank and honest answer. They are patriots. Don't mention the negative sides of the country (e.g. the situation of racial minorities, Vietnam war, Gulf war). Think positive!
- Avoid religion and politics.
- Avoid smoking.
- Don't get too close to them. Give them space.
- They like to do business while eating. Time is money.

4. SMALL TALK in France

They don't small talk at meetings which is so typical of the Americans or the British. Neither is humour used to break the ice or to warm up the audience. So do not sprinkle your presentation with jokes, because business is a serious matter.

Mind your manners

- The French are proud of their language and prefer to speak it with guests from abroad. Even if your French is bad, it helps to break down barriers.
- The French are formal and may be seen as cold and aloof. Use Monsieur and Madame regularly. Stay warm and friendly without getting over-familiar.
- Avoid conversation openers that are popular in England, Germany and the States: "What do you do for a living?", "Are you married?", "Do you have children?". Keep to the Tour de France, their excellent food or discuss art and culture, if you are a master of the subject. If not, you can score points by criticising the English – a favourite French pastime.

➡ Taboo subjects: never mention the War and don't bring up the subject of the German Occupation. The French do not accept that they were defeated.

➡ The French tend to butt in on each other's conversations. This is not rudeness, but proof that they are listening and interested in taking part.

➡ French people believe that there is more to life than the job. Eating is part of the secret of good life. They honour guests at the best restaurants with three to six-course meals. An American who talks business to a Frenchman over dinner will find his French colleague wants to enjoy his meal. They do not admire workaholics, so don't talk business over lunch.

5. SMALL TALK in Portugal

If the Portuguese people were not very different from the Spanish, Portugal would not exist. The Portuguese are an Atlantic nation, the Spanish are a Mediterranean nation. Until the 1974 revolution Portugal looked towards Africa (Angola, Mozambique) and South Africa.

Contrary to the Mediterranean peoples they are good speakers of the English language. Meetings normally start with some small talk.

Mind your manners

➡ They are not so touchy about race or religion as the Spanish. They are not so emotional as the Italians or the Spanish.

➡ They are more formal than the Spanish. They address anyone who appears qualified or intelligent as Duotor or Engenheiro.

➡ Don't ask questions about the revolution, don't praise their neighbour, Spain.

➡ Keep to the beauty of the country and their successful football team Benefica Lisboa.

➡ They avoid conflicts with colleagues and business partners.

➡ They are friendly, cheerful and communicative even at the beginning of a relationship.

6. SMALL TALK in Spain

Demonstrate interest in the country's history and culture. If you don't care for bullfighting and it comes up in conversation, avoid criticising. The Spanish consider it an art to confront a massive animal that has been trained to kill man by holding a little sword and a red cape. The typical English fox hunt is seen as a cowardly sport: the ladies and gentlemen sit safely astride a horse while thirty dogs tear a small fox to pieces.

Mind your manners

→ Shake hands when first meeting. Wait for a woman to offer her hand first.

→ Don't try to do business during afternoon siesta. Business lunch starts at about 13.30 and can last until 17.00. Dinner is between 22.00 and 23.00. Be careful not to get drunk. Dress conservatively.

→ If invited to the home, a gift is not expected, but you may bring a box of candy. Do not send flowers except for special occasions.

One peninsula – two nations

Spain	Portugal
The Spanish are a Mediterranean nation.	The Portuguese are an Atlantic nation.
They think the Iberian Peninsula is Spanish.	They see the Spanish as potential invaders.
They are less formal. They use the *tu* form all over the place.	They are more formal. They use titles.
Personal dignity is more important than time or money. Do not make them lose face.	National honour, race, religion are not major factors.
They are "machos".	They are less robust.
They like physical and eye contact.	They are more reserved.

7. **SMALL TALK** in Russia

Russian are searchers of their Slavic souls. That is why other people some-times find their Russian partners sentimental and gloomy. Conversation is rarely trivial. Within minutes, the subject is the meaning of life.

Mind your manners

▶ Introductions are informal and direct. A smile is only used for greeting personal friends. Smiling is not respectful on formal occasions and smiling for no reason is a sign of idiocy.

▶ Shake hands when first meeting people and leaving, but never across a threshold. It is a sign of bad luck.

▶ Russians are still very title-conscious: use titles and show respect.

▶ Russians think of themselves as being absolutely honest and trustworthy. So don't show distrust.

▶ Like most nations they are proud of their country. Don't tell them that in your country everything is bigger, cleaner and better organised.

▶ If you are invited to a Russian home, it is customary to bring flowers, vodka or wine.

▶ Dinner is eaten early, about six o'clock or whenever they feel hungry.

▶ Toasts are common, and the guest must be prepared to return toasts.

▶ Among younger businessmen you will find more and more non-smo-kers, teetotallers and even vegetarians. Invitations could include a ballet, circus or concert and dinner in a restaurant.

Russians are puzzled that westerners can spend the equivalent of an annual salary in Moscow hotels and restaurants, but are unwilling to give them a fax machine so that they can communicate more easily.

8. SMALL TALK in Japan

The basis of Japanese business etiquette is mutual trust and respect for individuals, companies and values.

Mind your manners

▶ The Japanese do not shake hands; making physical contact is an uncomfortable experience. If they offer handshakes to westerners it should be followed by a slight bow of your head. The grip should be gentle. Imitate your host.

▶ Do not look them straight in the eyes. It can appear challenging and makes them feel uncomfortable.

▶ When you are introduced give them your business card. Cards are also exchanged at parties. You might need up to 30 cards a day. Your cards should be in English and Japanese. You need a qualified professional translator to get it done properly.

▶ When offered a business card, do not put it in your pocket. Read it immediately and leave it in front of you on the table.

▶ When talking to the Japanese keep a greater distance than at home. And do not point with your finger, it is impolite.

▶ Be aware of silences or gaps in the conversation and don't make the western mistake of trying to fill them; silence is "golden" after all.

▶ They are highly status-conscious. Top level executives expect to do business with top level managers from the other company. It is a sign of respect. Never use first names.

▶ They enjoy giving carefully chosen personal gifts. Westerners are often surprised at the trouble they take to find out about a visitor's family. Follow their example when they visit you.

▶ The Japanese Samurai feels uncomfortable in the presence of clever businesswomen who try to negotiate in an aggressive way. Women are rarely invited into the men's social circles.

▶ Dress conservatively: blue or grey suit, white shirt, dark tie. They like clean, not too young, not too hairy, calm and modest business partners.

9. SMALL TALK in China

Westerners see China as a Third World underdeveloped country. They forget that it is also the oldest civilisation on earth that invented gun powder and porcelain at a time when Europeans were still throwing stones at each other. They have civilised Japan and all their neighbouring nations. They see themselves as the middle Empire, the centre of the universe, which might become the planet's biggest future market. They do not trust us westerners who in some parts of China are still considered as "foreign devils".

Be patient when doing business in China – how patient this story will illustrate.

A young Chinese was called to his boss who was to retire soon. The old man asked him if he was ready to take his position in the communist party. The young man was overjoyed. "One thing you must remember when dealing with people," said the old man, "always be patient." The young man nodded. The old man repeated his advice three times, when he was going to repeat it a fourth time, the young man said "Do you take me for an idiot? Why do you repeat such a simple thing four times?" And the old man smiled and said "I've said it a few times, and you are already impatient."

Mind your manners

- ➡ Offer gifts in private, not in front of others, as in Arab countries.
- ➡ Don't imitate your Chinese partners. Be yourself!
- ➡ Don't show off your knowledge of Chinese culture and traditions even if you think you are an expert on Chinese affairs. (By the way, you are not and will never be one.) They might interpret it as western arrogance.
- ➡ Be modest! Make excuses that you don't know much about their culture. They will forgive you.
- ➡ In China a wise man knows when to shut up. Don't talk too much!
- ➡ When an Asian smiles it could be a signal that he is embarrassed about some bad news.
- ➡ If a toast is made, there will be a clapping of hands. Clap back and smile.
- ➡ Don't refuse food or drinks. Your host will be offended. Learn to eat with chopsticks. Don't be afraid – it's a good omen if you drop them on the floor.

➡ Don't refer to China as Mainland China. It is the People's Republic of China. And Taiwan is not a sovereign state but one of the Republic's provinces.

➡ Learn a few words of Chinese to be able to make polite noises. It's good if you know enough Mandarin to understand what your partners and your interpreter say. Don't try to speak it, even if you are under the illusion that you can. They won't appreciate your accent.

In China time is relative, which the following story shows.
A Chinese official informed an ARCO manager that tomorrow China would be the number one nation in the world. The American said that he did not doubt it, considering the size of the country and its population, and the tremendous technical progress being made, but he asked, "When do you think that China will become number one?" The Chinese answered: "Oh, in four or five hundred years."

10. SMALL TALK in South Korea

Within the last 50 years South Korea has developed from an agricultural country to one of the new Tiger Economies. Korean society is highly structured; great respect is paid to age. They are Buddhists with a strong Confucian tradition.

Mind your manners

➡ When invited to a Korean home remove your shoes and wait to be invited inside.

➡ Don't knock at the door, it's a western tradition. Koreans find it intrusive. Cough or call out their names instead.

➡ They are on first-name terms only with people they know very well.

➡ Avoid topics like socialism, communism or Korean politics.

➡ At parties stay with your hosts or your group. Don't circulate on your own. At home, don't leave your Korean guests. Circulate with them.

➡ They tend to stand close to you when talking and touch your arm to attract attention.

➡ Don't be offended when a Korean asks: "Where are you going? What time are you going to eat? What's that book you're reading?" Smile and say something vague – that's what is expected.

- Be prepared for personal questions: "Are you married? How old are you? How much do you earn?"
- Conversation takes place after the meal, not during the meal.
- After a meal you say "I've eaten very well. It was really delicious." A mere "Thank you" is not enough. It sounds insincere.
- Smiles are reserved for personal relationships. Smiling at newcomers is considered to be to pushy.
- Laughter is a sign of embarrassment, a sort of apology after having committed a blunder.
- Don't scratch your nose. Finger to nose gestures are very rude. Keep your fingers away from your face.
- Saying "no" when offered something is a sign of politeness. Say no a couple of times and then accept. You don't have to eat, drink or smoke it.

11. SMALL TALK in Arab countries

The 21 states of the Arab League are an interesting market for European companies. These states cover a territory three times that of Europe and many are rich in oil. Their total population is over 200 million. No Arab constitution is older than 90 years. European managers do not think highly of Arab countries: "Where would they be without their oil?" The Arabs, however have not forgotten that they were once the leading civilisation in the western world. They try to strike a balance between modern technology and their traditions.

Mind your manners

- First, don't say anything to insult their country. They believe they were world leaders and can be again. Of course we just see them living off oil revenues. Don't say anything like that to them.
- Here in the West we are individual-oriented. They are centred on the family. So if you get the chance, wish members of the family the best. But not any of the females – don't compliment on the cooking. Take the women's work for granted. Or you'll be up to your neck in it.
- Arabs tend to come very close to you when speaking. They touch a lot as well. Don't move away if possible otherwise they'll feel you're being arrogant.

- Look them in the eye when talking to them. Eye contact counts for a lot. And try praising their country, art, dress and food (but not their women).
- Learn a few polite noises in Arabic.
- Accept all invitations.
- Give your gift in front of others so that there will be no appearance of bribery.
- Don't ask them to unpack a present in your presence.
- Take only the food that is offered to you.
- Eat with your right hand.
- Avoid unpleasant subjects like accidents, poverty, death.
- Leave soon after eating.
- Praise their country, food and fashion.
- Don't refer to the Gulf as the Persian Gulf. It is the Arab Gulf.
- Don't shake hands with women.
- Don't enquire about your host's wives or daughters.
- Don't discuss women, politics or religion.
- Don't admire your host's pictures, furniture or horses. He might feel obliged to give them to you as a present.
- Don't point the sole of the foot towards someone when seated.

You had better read the Koran if you want to do business with them. In the Gulf States a good manager is a good Moslem. He will often refer to Allah and the Koran. Islam influences every aspect in the Arab world especially in Saudi Arabia. The Third Development Plan for the Kingdom of Saudi Arabia, 1980–1985 clearly stated: "The distinguishing mark of the Saudi approach to development is that its material and social objectives are derived from the ethical principles of Islam and the cultural values of Saudi society." So your partners and you will often have different views of what is right or wrong.

They talk about other things before they talk about business. Then after having talked about business they might come back to social matters and so on. The Arab language is a poetic language, rich in associations and allusions. It is important for native speakers how they say what they mean. They tend to over-express themselves using exaggerations, fantastic metaphors, strings of adjectives and repetition accompanied by vivid body language. To the Arab loudness is a sign of strength and sincerity, soft tones imply weakness and a lack of sincerity. Remember, the Gulf War took place partly because George Bush spoke softly and Saddam Hussein did not believe what he said about declaring war.

SMALL-TALKER'S DICTIONARY

1. Starting a conversation with strangers
2. At a congress or a conference
3. Introducing yourself
4. Introducing others
5. Ice breakers
6. Be my guest
7. Feel at home
8. Conversation openers
9. Suggesting a toast
10. Making polite noises
11. Leave-taking
12. Small talk with people you know
13. Unlocking memories
14. Excuse me, can I have a word with you?
15. Finding common ground
16. Polite noises to make them talk
17. Building bridges
18. Showing one's sympathy
19. Taking a stand
20. Disagreeing
21. Exploring business opportunities

1. Starting a conversation with strangers

Excuse me, do you speak English?	*Entschuldigen Sie, sprechen Sie Englisch?*
Excuse me. May I ask you a question?	*Entschuldigen Sie. Darf ich Sie etwas fragen?*
Excuse me, is this seat taken?	*Entschuldigung, ist dieser Platz besetzt?*
Nasty weather, isn't it?	*Ein scheußliches Wetter, nicht wahr?*
What a slow train it is!	*Das ist aber ein langsamer Zug!*
I beg your pardon. Was that your glass /chair?	*Entschuldigung, war das Ihr Glas / Stuhl?*
I am awfully sorry, was that your foot?	*Tut mir furchtbar Leid. War das Ihr Fuß?*
You look worried. Is there anything I can do for you?	*Sie sehen besorgt aus. Kann ich irgendetwas für Sie tun?*
Has it been raining here like this for long?	*Regnet es so schon lange hier?*
It's rather cold / hot / crowded in here, don't you think?	*Es ist ziemlich kalt /heiß / voll hier, finden Sie nicht auch?*
May I invite you for a drink?	*Darf ich Sie zu einem Drink einladen?*
Why not have a beer? – Good idea!	*Wie wär's mit einem Bier? – Gute Idee!*
Is this your first visit to Germany?	*Sind Sie zum ersten Mal in Deutschland?*
Are you here on business or pleasure?	*Sind Sie geschäftlich hier oder zum Vergnügen?*

2. At a congress or a conference

Excuse me, where is the conference room?	*Entschuldigen Sie, wo ist das Konferenzzimmer?*
Are you here for the first time? – So am I.	*Sind Sie zum ersten Mal hier? – Ich auch.*
You look a bit lost. Can I help you?	*Sie sehen ein bisschen verloren aus. Kann ich Ihnen helfen?*
Nice place. Do you come here often?	*Es ist nett hier. Kommen Sie oft hierher?*
I'm from Germany. Where are you from?	*Ich bin aus Deutschland. Wo kommen Sie her?*

Do you happen to know the guest speaker?	*Kennen Sie den Gastredner?*
What do you expect from this congress?	*Was erwarten Sie von dem Kongress?*
Are you here on business?	*Sind Sie geschäftlich hier?*
Can I get you a drink?	*Kann ich Ihnen etwas zu trinken anbieten?*
May I ask why you are here?	*Darf ich fragen, warum Sie hier sind?*
Are you also staying at the Hilton?	*Sind Sie auch im Hilton?*
Is it comfortable? – Yes, very.	*Ist es angenehm? – Ja, sehr.*
What's the food like?	*Wie ist das Essen?*
How long are you staying? – Only for two days.	*Wie lange bleiben Sie? – Nur für zwei Tage.*
Here is my card.	*Hier ist meine Visitenkarte.*
We could have dinner together, if you like.	*Wir könnten zusammen zu Abend essen, wenn Sie wollen.*

3. Introducing yourself

By the way, my name is Meier.	*Übrigens, ich heiße Meier.*
Perhaps I should introduce myself.	*Ich sollte mich vielleicht vorstellen.*
Tom Dobson's the name.	*Mein Name ist Tom Dobson.*
I am from Bonn. Where do you come from?	*Ich bin aus Bonn. Wo kommen Sie her?*
I am here on a holiday/business trip.	*Ich bin auf Urlaub/Geschäftsreise hier.*
Pleased to meet you.	*Freut mich, Sie kennen zu lernen.*
Happy to make your acquaintance.	*Ich freue mich, Ihre Bekanntschaft zu machen.*
I think we've met before.	*Ich glaube, wir sind uns schon einmal begegnet.*
Do you remember me? We met at Tom Green's party last week.	*Erinnern Sie sich an mich? Wir haben uns auf Tom Greens Party kennengelernt.*
Pleased to meet you.	*Freut mich, Sie kennen zu lernen.*
Glad to meet you, too.	*Ganz meinerseits.*

4. Introducing others

Mr Pitt, may I introduce you to Mrs Bell?	*Mr Pitt, darf ich Ihnen Mrs Bell vorstellen?*
Paul, I'd like you to meet Peter. Peter, this is Paul.	*Paul, ich möchte dich mit Peter bekannt machen. Paul, das ist Peter.*
Tom, I'm not sure if have you met Paul. Paul, this is Tom.	*Paul, ich weiß nicht, ob du Peter schon kennst. Peter, das ist Paul.*
Pleased to meet you.	*Freut mich, Sie kennen zu lernen.*
The pleasure is mine.	*Ganz meinerseits.*

5. Ice-breakers

Did you have a good journey?	*Hatten Sie eine angenehme Reise?*
Had a good journey, I hope.	*Hoffentlich hatten Sie eine gute Reise.*
The train was rather overcrowded.	*Der Zug war ziemlich überfüllt.*
I hope you had a pleasant flight.	*Ich hoffe, Sie hatten einen guten Flug.*
The flight was rather bumpy.	*Der Flug war ziemlich unruhig.*
Did you get through the customs okay?	*Sind Sie gut durch den Zoll gekommen?*
I didn't have any problems.	*Es ist alles glatt gegangen.*
How was the transfer to the hotel?	*Wie war der Transfer zum Hotel?*
We haven't seen each other for ages.	*Wir haben uns ja schon eine Ewigkeit nicht mehr gesehen.*
How are your wife and children?	*Wie geht es Frau und Kindern?*
By the way, many thanks for your Christmas greetings.	*Übrigens vielen Dank für Ihre Weihnachtsgrüße.*
Thanks for your card when you were on holiday.	*Vielen Dank für Ihre Karte aus dem Urlaub.*
Did you find our company straight away?	*Haben Sie unsere Firma gleich gefunden?*
I didn't have any trouble thanks to your clear instructions.	*Dank Ihrer genauen Beschreibung hatte ich keine Probleme.*
Let's sit down, shall we?	*Aber bitte, setzen wir uns doch.*
May I introduce you?	*Darf ich bekannt machen?*
Let's forget the formalities.	*Lassen wir die Förmlichkeiten beiseite.*
I suggest we drop the formalities.	*Ich schlage vor, wir lassen die Förmlichkeiten beiseite.*

May I offer you something to drink? Coffee, tea or something else?	Darf ich Ihnen etwas zum Trinken anbieten? Kaffee, Tee oder sonst etwas?
I'll have the same as you.	Ich nehme das Gleiche wie Sie.
Do you feel like talking business right now?	Ist es Ihnen recht, wenn wir gleich über das Geschäftliche sprechen?
Shall we have a drop of something to keep the cold out?	Trinken wir ein Schnäpschen zum Aufwärmen?

6. Be my guest

What are you doing this evening?	Was haben Sie heute Abend vor?
I am thinking of having a quiet evening.	Ich möchte einen geruhsamen Abend verbringen.
Have you got anything planned for tonight?	Haben Sie schon etwas für heute Abend vor?
Would you like to join us for dinner this evening?	Möchten Sie heute Abend zu uns zum Essen kommen?
Thank you, that sounds very nice.	Vielen Dank, das ist sehr nett von Ihnen.
I would be pleased if you would honour me with your company.	Ich würde mich freuen, wenn Sie mir Gesellschaft leisten würden.
May I invite you to my place tonight?	Darf ich Sie heute Abend zu mir einladen?
Would you and your wife like to come over for a glass of wine?	Hätten Sie und Ihre Frau Lust, auf ein Glas Wein zu uns zu kommen?
I'd love to; at what time?	Gerne, um wie viel Uhr?
Would between eight and half past suit you?	Passt es Ihnen zwischen acht und halb neun?
We've invited a few colleagues over for Friday evening. Wouldn't you like to join us, too?	Wir haben ein paar Kollegen für Freitagabend eingeladen. Möchten Sie nicht dazukommen?
I'd love to, but unfortunately I won't be able to. Our sales manager is coming for the weekend.	Ich würde gerne kommen, aber leider kann ich nicht. Unser Verkaufsmanager kommt zum Wochenende.
I'd love to, but I've got an another engagement.	Ich würde sehr gerne, aber ich habe schon eine Verpflichtung.
Why don't you bring your colleague along with you?	Warum bringen Sie Ihren Kollegen nicht mit?

My wife would like to meet you.	*Meine Frau würde Sie gerne kennen lernen.*
I'm afraid I can't make it tonight.	*Ich kann leider heute Abend nicht.*
She'll be very depressed if you turn us down.	*Sie wird sehr traurig sein, wenn Sie es uns abschlagen.*
She'll be very disappointed if you refuse our invitation.	*Sie wird sehr enttäuscht sein, wenn Sie unsere Einladung ablehnen.*
Thank you very much. I'll look forward to that.	*Vielen Dank. Ich komme gerne.*
I'm looking forward to meeting your family.	*Ich freue mich darauf, Ihre Familie kennen zu lernen.*
I'm afraid I'll have to say no – I need an early night.	*Ich fürchte, ich muss ablehnen. Ich muss mal wieder früh ins Bett.*

7. Feel at home

Please, come on in.	*Aber bitte, kommen Sie doch herein.*
It's good to see you here again.	*Schön, dich wieder bei uns zu haben.*
Do you want to take your coat off?	*Wollen Sie nicht ablegen?*
May I take your coat?	*Darf ich Ihnen Ihren Mantel abnehmen?*
Do sit down.	*Aber setzen Sie sich doch.*
Have a seat.	*Nehmen Sie Platz.*
Can I offer you a drink?	*Kann ich Ihnen etwas zu trinken anbieten?*
May I offer you an aperitif?	*Darf ich Ihnen einen Aperitif anbieten?*
Would you like a sherry?	*Möchten Sie einen Sherry?*
Help yourself to some more.	*Gießen Sie sich noch etwas ein.*
The bar is over there. Please help yourself.	*Die Bar ist dort drüben. Bitte bedienen Sie sich.*
Excuse me, where is the toilet, please?	*Entschuldigen Sie, wo ist bitte die Toilette?*
You've got a cosy flat.	*Sie haben eine gemütliche Wohnung.*
You have a wonderful house.	*Sie haben ein wundervolles Haus.*
Would you like me to show you around the house?	*Möchten Sie, dass ich Ihnen das Haus zeige?*
What a nice garden you have!	*Was für ein schöner Garten!*

Let's go and sit in the garden.	*Setzen wir uns noch etwas in den Garten.*
I'd like to live in the country, too.	*Ich würde auch gerne auf dem Land leben.*
May I introduce you to my wife?	*Darf ich Sie mit meiner Frau bekannt machen?*
I've brought you a little something.	*Ich habe Ihnen eine Kleinigkeit mitgebracht.*
Thank you. You shouldn't have.	*Herzlichen Dank. Aber das war doch nicht nötig.*
My husband has told me a lot about you.	*Mein Mann hat mir schon viel von Ihnen erzählt.*
Only good things, I hope.	*Ich hoffe, nur Gutes.*
Make yourself at home.	*Fühlen Sie sich ganz wie zu Hause.*

8. Conversation openers

Did you find us straight away?	*Haben Sie uns gleich gefunden?*
I came by taxi.	*Ich bin mit dem Taxi gekommen.*
When did you arrive?	*Wann sind Sie angekommen?*
Have you been to England before?	*Waren Sie schon mal in England?*
How long have you been in England?	*Wie lange sind Sie schon in England?*
I've been in England for three days.	*Ich bin seit drei Tagen in England.*
Do you like your accommodation?	*Sind Sie gut untergebracht?*
Are you satisfied with your hotel?	*Sind Sie mit Ihrem Hotel zufrieden?*
Have you adjusted to life here yet?	*Haben Sie sich schon eingelebt?*
Yes, everybody here is very helpful.	*Ja, alle hier sind sehr hilfsbereit.*
How has your stay in England been so far?	*Wie war Ihr Aufenthalt in England bis jetzt?*
I've been enjoying every single day.	*Ich genieße jeden einzelnen Tag.*
How do you like our town?	*Wie gefällt Ihnen unsere Stadt?*
The people are all really friendly.	*Die Menschen sind alle ausgesprochen freundlich.*
I haven't had time yet to walk around the city.	*Ich habe noch keine Zeit für einen Stadtbummel gefunden.*
The ancient city is really marvellous.	*Die Altstadt ist wirklich wundervoll.*
How are you finding things in Germany?	*Wie gefällt es Ihnen in Deutschland?*

It's a bit early to form an opinion.	*Ich kann noch nicht viel darüber sagen.*
Are you from here originally?	*Stammen Sie aus dieser Gegend?*
I'm from York. I moved here about 20 years ago.	*Ich bin aus York. Ich bin vor 20 Jahren hierher gezogen.*
York? Whereabouts is that?	*Wo liegt York?*
Dinner is ready. Let's move to the living-room.	*Das Essen ist fertig. Gehen wir ins Wohnzimmer.*
We can continue our conversation at dinner.	*Wir können uns beim Essen weiter unterhalten.*

9. Suggesting a toast

Cheers!	*Prost!*
To your good health!	*Auf Ihr Wohl!*
I'd like to propose a toast to the conclusion of our contract.	*Ich schlage vor, wir trinken auf den Abschluss unseres Vertrags.*
Let's raise our glasses to the future of Europe.	*Erheben wir unsere Gläser, und trinken wir auf die Zukunft Europas.*
I rise to toast our guests.	*Ich erhebe mich, um auf das Wohl unserer Gäste zu trinken.*
I'd like to make a toast to our new colleague.	*Ich möchte einen Toast auf unseren neuen Kollegen ausbringen.*
Ladies and gentlemen, let's celebrate this with a glass of champagne.	*Meine Damen und Herren, begießen wir es mit einem Glas Champagner.*
Here's to the beautiful bride.	*Auf das Wohl der schönen Braut.*
I want to wish the newly wed couple all the best.	*Ich wünsche dem neuvermählten Paar alles Gute.*
Best of luck, you two. And now everybody, bottoms up!	*Viel Glück, euch beiden. Und nun, hoch die Tassen!*

10. Making polite noises

I hadn't expected such a good dinner.	*Auf ein so gutes Abendessen war ich nicht gefasst.*
That was really excellent.	*Das war wirklich ausgezeichnet.*
You must let me have the recipe.	*Sie müssen mir das Rezept geben.*
What a beautiful garden you have!	*Was für einen hübschen Garten Sie haben!*
I must say you certainly know what's what.	*Ich muss wirklich sagen, du verstehst zu leben.*
I have heard a lot about your stamp collection.	*Ich habe viel von Ihrer Briefmarkensammlung gehört.*
I quite fancy your collection of arms.	*Mir gefällt Ihre Waffensammlung wirklich sehr.*
That's second to none!	*Das ist einmalig!*
It's out of this world!	*Das ist absolute Spitze!*
I'd like to begin by congratulating Tom on his performance.	*Ich möchte zu Beginn Tom zu seiner Leistung gratulieren.*
Well done!	*Gut gemacht!*
Full marks!	*Volltreffer!*
Not bad at all!	*Gar nicht schlecht!*
Good for you!	*Bravo!*
That's a touch of perfection!	*Das ist meisterhaft!*

11. Leave-taking

Goodness, is it that time already?	*Mein Gott, ist es schon so spät?*
I'm afraid I've got to leave now.	*Ich fürchte, ich muss nun gehen.*
I've got a train to catch.	*Ich muss meinen Zug erreichen.*
But you've only just arrived.	*Aber Sie sind doch gerade erst gekommen.*
Such a shame you have to go already.	*Wie schade, dass Sie schon gehen müssen. Nun, ich will Sie nicht aufhalten.*
Well, I mustn't keep you.	
I think I should be going now.	*Ich glaube, ich sollte langsam aufbrechen.*
I'm afraid I must be going now.	*Ich muss mich nun leider verabschieden.*

I don't want to overstay my welcome.	*Ich möchte Ihre Gastfreundschaft nicht überstrapazieren.*
I really can't stay any longer.	*Ich kann wirklich nicht länger bleiben.*
You're not thinking of going already?	*Sie wollen doch nicht etwa schon gehen?*
I'm afraid I must be setting off now.	*Ich fürchte, ich muss mich langsam auf den Weg machen.*
Do you really have to go already?	*Müssen Sie wirklich schon gehen?*
Tomorrow is going to be a hard day for me.	*Ich habe morgen einen anstrengenden Tag vor mir.*
It's already late and we've to make an early start tomorrow morning.	*Es ist schon spät, und wir alle müssen morgen wieder früh raus.*
It's been a delightful evening.	*Es war ein bezaubernder Abend.*
Thanks so much for the delightful evening.	*Vielen herzlichen Dank für den netten Abend.*
Thank you ever so much. This has been a most pleasant evening.	*Vielen Dank. Es war ein sehr schöner Abend.*
Glad you enjoyed it.	*Schön, dass es Ihnen gefallen hat.*
Thank you so much for the superb dinner.	*Vielen Dank für das ausgezeichnete Abendessen.*
Don't mention it. We hope you enjoyed yourself.	*Keine Ursache. Wir hoffen, es hat Ihnen gefallen.*
I'm sorry you can't stay a bit longer.	*Ich finde es schade, dass Sie nicht länger bleiben können.*
It's a pity you can't stay.	*Schade, dass Sie nicht bleiben können.*
We hope to hear from you soon.	*Wir hoffen, bald wieder von Ihnen zu hören.*
I trust we'll see each other again before too long.	*Ich hoffe, wir sehen uns in naher Zukunft wieder.*
You must soon come and see us again.	*Sie müssen uns bald wieder besuchen kommen.*
Can I see you home, perhaps?	*Kann ich Sie vielleicht nach Hause begleiten?*
May I give you a lift to your hotel?	*Darf ich Sie zu Ihrem Hotel fahren?*

12. Small talk with people you know

If you aren't expecting anybody, do you mind if I join you?	*Darf ich mich zu Ihnen setzen, falls Sie niemanden erwarten?*
Hello Tom. I haven't see you for ages.	*Hallo, Tom. Ich habe dich eine Ewigkeit nicht gesehen.*
How has life been treating you?	*Wie geht's dir so?*
How are you these days?	*Wie geht's dir so?*
How are you keeping nowadays?	*Wie geht's dir so?*
How are we this morning?	*Wie geht's uns heute morgen?*
Fine, thank you. And you?	*Danke, gut. Und wie geht's dir?*
It could be worse.	*Es könnte mir schlimmer gehen.*
I can't complain.	*Ich kann nicht klagen.*
I have nothing to complain about.	*Es gibt nichts, worüber ich klagen könnte.*
I'm getting on nicely.	*Mir geht's gut.*
I'm feeling great.	*Mir geht es großartig.*
I feel on top of the world.	*Mir geht es bestens.*
I couldn't feel better.	*Es könnte mir nicht besser gehen.*
I don't really want to waste your time with that now.	*Ich will eigentlich gar nicht deine Zeit damit verschwenden.*
I hope you're settling in at your new job.	*Ich hoffe, du gewöhnst dich allmählich an deinen neuen Job.*
Tell me about your holiday in ...	*Erzähl mir von deinem Urlaub in ...*
Have you still got your BMW?	*Hast du immer noch deinen BMW?*
Where are you off to next?	*Wohin fährst du als Nächstes?*
Have you ever visited Boston?	*Warst du schon mal in Boston?*
How is your new boss?	*Wie ist dein neuer Chef?*
Let's not talk business.	*Reden wir nicht vom Geschäft.*

13. Unlocking memories

How long have we known each other?	*Wie lange kennen wir uns jetzt schon?*
That must be a good ten years.	*Das müssen gut und gerne 10 Jahre sein.*
By the way, this reminds me of the day of when we first met.	*Ach, das erinnert mich übrigens an den Tag, als wir uns zum ersten Mal begegnet sind.*
That must have been ages ago.	*Das muss eine Ewigkeit her sein. Wo war das doch gleich wieder?*
Wasn't that at Tom's party?	*War das nicht auf Toms Party?*
No, I think it was in Professor X's lecture on ...	*Nein, ich glaube das war in der Vorlesung über ... von Professor X.*
I can't remember any of that at all.	*Daran kann ich mich überhaupt nicht mehr erinnern.*
Can't you really remember?	*Erinnerst du dich wirklich nicht mehr?*
Oh yes, it's gradually coming back to me?	*Ach ja, jetzt fällt es mir langsam wieder ein.*
Now it's beginning to dawn on me.	*Jetzt dämmert es mir wieder.*
Those were the days.	*Das waren noch Zeiten.*
Do you still think about our days in Paris?	*Denkst du noch manchmal an unsere Zeit in Paris?*
In those days we were young and eager.	*Damals waren wir noch jung und unternehmungslustig.*
I'll never forget how you helped me out of that tight spot.	*Ich werde nie vergessen, wie du mir aus der Patsche geholfen hast.*
I'll never forget our holiday together.	*Unser gemeinsamer Urlaub ist mir unvergesslich.*
I'll remember our student days well.	*Ich erinnere mich noch gut an unsere Studienzeit.*
Do you remember how we celebrated our first job together?	*Weißt du noch, wie wir zusammen unseren ersten Job gefeiert haben?*
Can you remember old Dobson?	*Erinnerst du dich noch an den alten Dobson?*
Wasn't that the landlady from the Red Lion?	*War das nicht die Wirtin vom Roten Löwen?*
If I'm not mistaken you were after her.	*Wenn mich nicht alles täuschst, warst du hinter ihr her.*

What a memory you've got!	*Dein Gedächtnis möchte ich haben.*
Are you still in contact with Tony?	*Hast du noch Kontakt mit Tony?*
Tony, the rat. How could I forget him?	*Tony, die Ratte. Wie könnte ich den vergessen?*
Is he still as boring as he was?	*Ist er immer noch so langweilig?*
Whatever happened to long-legged Jane?	*Was ist eigentlich aus der langbeingen Jane geworden?*
It's nice to remember old times.	*Es tut gut, die alten Erinnerungen wieder aufzufrischen.*
We really must see each other again.	*Wir müssen uns unbedingt mal wieder treffen.*

14. Excuse me, can I have a word with you?

Do you remember me? We met at a Robinson Club.	*Erinnern Sie sich an mich? Wir haben uns in einem Robinson Club getroffen.*
Yes, I do, but I'm afraid I didn't recognise you at first.	*Sicher, aber ich habe Sie nicht gleich wiedererkannt.*
We weren't introduced formally introduced then.	*Wir sind uns damals nicht offiziell bekannt gemacht worden.*
Are you here for the first time?	*Sind Sie zum ersten Mal hier?*
How long have you known our host?	*Wie lange kennen Sie schon unseren Gastgeber?*
Who else do you know at the party?	*Wen kennen Sie sonst noch auf dieser Party?*
Excuse me, can I have a word with you?	*Entschuldigen Sie, kann ich Sie kurz sprechen?*
I'd like to have a word with you, if you've got the time.	*Ich würde Sie gerne sprechen, wenn Sie einen Augenblick Zeit haben.*
I'd really appreciate a moment of your time.	*Ich wäre Ihnen wirklich dankbar, wenn Sie einen Augenblick für mich Zeit hätten.*
Have you got a moment? I'd like to ask you a question.	*Haben Sie einen Moment Zeit? Ich würde Sie gerne etwas fragen.*
I won't keep you very long if you are in a hurry.	*Ich werde Sie nicht lange aufhalten, wenn Sie es eilig haben.*
I've something important to discuss with you.	*Ich habe etwas Wichtiges mit Ihnen zu besprechen.*

15. Finding common ground

Are you married, too?	*Sind Sie auch verheiratet?*
Do you have a family?	*Haben Sie Familie?*
Do you have children, too?	*Haben Sie auch Kinder?*
What a coincidence! My family is from Switzerland, too?	*Was für ein Zufall! Meine Familie stammt auch aus der Schweiz.*
We both play tennis. We could play doubles some time.	*Wir spielen beide Tennis. Wir könnten mal ein Doppel machen.*
I've heard you're good at chess. What about us having a game?	*Ich habe gehört, Sie sind ein guter Schachspieler. Wie wär's mit einer Partie Schach?*
We seem to have a hobby in common.	*Offensichtlich haben wir ein gemeinsames Hobby.*
I met Tom yesterday. He sends his best regards.	*Ich habe gestern Tom getroffen. Er lässt Sie herzlich grüßen.*
Do there happen to be other doctors in this room?	*Sind hier vielleicht noch andere Ärzte in diesem Raum?*
We seem to be in the same business.	*Wir scheinen in der gleichen Branche zu sein.*
I sell cars, too.	*Ich verkaufe auch Autos.*
I was sent here by my boss.	*Mich hat mein Chef hierher geschickt.*
Why are you here?	*Warum sind Sie hier?*
I drive a Rover. I saw you arrive in the same car. Are you happy with it?	*Ich fahre einen Rover. Ich sah Sie in dem gleichen Auto kommen. Sind Sie zufrieden damit?*

16. Polite noises to make them talk

Hmm, I see.	*Aha! Ich verstehe.*
Tell me more.	*Erzählen Sie mir mehr davon.*
Would you believe it!	*Kaum zu glauben!*
Do you really mean that?	*Ist das wirklich Ihr Ernst?*
You don't say!	*Was Sie nicht sagen!*
That's most interesting.	*Das ist höchst interessant.*
I'd never have believed it.	*Hätte ich nie geglaubt.*

17. Building bridges

That reminds me of a story I heard the other day.	*Das erinnert mich an eine Geschichte, die ich neulich gehört habe.*
When you mentioned Tom, I remembered how I first met him.	*Als du Tom erwähnt hast, habe ich mich erinnert, wie ich ihn das erste Mal getroffen habe.*
I had a similar experience a couple of years ago. It was in ...	*Ich hatte ein ähnliches Erlebnis vor ein paar Jahren. Es war in ...*
Talking about holidays, what are your plans for this year?	*Apropos Urlaub. Wie sind deine Pläne für dieses Jahr?*
Speaking of novels, what was the title of the one you recommended me?	*Da wir gerade von Romanen sprechen, wie war der Titel, den du mir empfohlen hast?*
Judging from what you say, you seem to read a lot, don't you?	*Wenn man Ihnen so zuhört, scheinen Sie viel zu lesen.*

18. Showing one's sympathy

I missed the plane. – Oh, bad luck.	*Ich habe das Flugzeug verpasst. – Ach, so ein Pech.*
I didn't get that job. – Well, better luck next time.	*Ich habe die Stelle nicht bekommen. – Na, das nächste Mal hast du mehr Glück.*
My boss died last week – I'm sorry to hear that.	*Mein Chef ist letzte Woche gestorben. – Es tut mir Leid, das zu hören*
It's a great loss to us all.	*Es ist für uns alle ein großer Verlust.*
I know what it is like.	*Ich weiß, wie das ist.*
I can imagine how you must feel.	*Ich kann mir vorstellen, wie Sie sich fühlen.*
I don't know what to say.	*Ich weiß gar nicht, was ich dazu sagen soll.*
Please accept my sympathy.	*Darf ich Ihnen meine Anteilnahme aussprechen?*

19. Taking a stand

If you ask me ...	*Wenn Sie mich fragen ...*
I'd say that ...	*Ich würde sagen, dass ...*
I presume ...	*Ich nehme an, dass ...*
I feel that ... / I think that ...	*Ich meine, dass ...*
I believe that ...	*Ich glaube, dass ...*
Well, of course I'm no expert on ... but I thought ...	*Nun, ich bin natürlich kein Fachmann für ..., aber ich dachte ...*
I, for my part, would say that ...	*Nun, was mich angeht, so würde ich sagen ...*
As far as I'm able to judge ...	*Soweit ich dies beurteilen kann ...*
It seems to me that ...	*Mir scheint, dass ...*
It appears to me as if ...	*Mir scheint, als ob ...*
I tend to think that ...	*Ich neige zu der Ansicht, dass ...*
If you want to know my opinion, I'd say that	*Wenn Sie meine Meinung wissen wollen, ich würde sagen, dass ...*
In my view / In my opinion ...	*Meiner Meinung nach ...*
As I see it ...	*Wie ich es / die Sache sehe ...*
As far as I'm concerned, I think that ...	*Was mich anbelangt, so glaube ich, dass ...*
I'm quite sure that ...	*Ich bin ziemlich sicher, dass ...*
I'm certain that ...	*Ich bin sicher, dass ...*
I'm convinced that ...	*Ich bin überzeugt, dass ...*
It is my conviction, that ...	*Es ist meine Überzeugung, dass ...*
It's my firm belief that ...	*Es ist meine feste Überzeugung, dass ...*

20. Disagreeing

I'm afraid ...	*Leider; ich fürchte ...*
Are you sure?	*Sind Sie sicher?*
I'm not so sure.	*Ich bin mir da nicht so sicher.*
Do you really think so?	*Meinen Sie wirklich?*
I'm not totally convinced.	*Ich bin nicht ganz davon überzeugt.*
I've got some reservations.	*Ich habe einige Bedenken.*
To a certain extent I agree with you, but I'm not totally convinced.	*Ich stimme mit Ihnen bis zu einem gewissen Grad überein, bin aber nicht völlig überzeugt.*

I don't quite agree with you.	*Ich bin nicht ganz Ihrer Meinung.*
I'm afraid I can't quite agree with you.	*Ich kann Ihnen leider nicht zustimmen.*
With respect, I see it a little differently.	*Nehmen Sie es mir nicht übel, aber ich sehe es etwas anders.*
I can't help feeling that I must disagree.	*Ich kann leider nicht umhin, anderer Meinung zu sein.*
To be honest, I can't share your opinion.	*Ehrlich gesagt, ich kann Ihre Meinung nicht teilen.*

21. Exploring business opportunities

You seem to know a lot about these things.	*Sie scheinen eine Menge darüber zu wissen*
Is this one of your hobbies?	*Ist das eines Ihrer Hobbys?*
You seem to be an expert on	*Sie scheinen ein Experte in ... zu sein.*
You must have a lot of experience with ...	*Sie müssen viel Erfahrung haben mit ...*
You are the most well-connected person I know. That reminds me, you don't happen to know a good address for ...?	*Ich kenne niemanden mit besseren Verbindungen wie Sie. Dabei fällt mir ein, kennen Sie zufällig eine gute Adresse für ...?*
By the way, if you come across someone who has a castle to sell, please let me know.	*Übrigens, wenn Sie jemanden treffen, der ein Schloss zu verkaufen hat, lassen Sie es mich bitte wissen.*
Does anybody else collect beer mats by any chance?	*Sammelt vielleicht noch jemand zufällig Bierdeckel?*
Bryan mentioned that you might be able to recommend a good supplier for office equipment.	*Bryan erwähnte, dass Sie mir vielleicht einen guten Lieferanten für Büromöbel empfehlen könnten.*
Obviously our business interests overlap in some areas.	*Unsere Geschäftsinteressen scheinen sich zu überlappen.*
I think this is in my interests as well as in yours.	*Ich glaube, das ist in meinem und in Ihrem Interesse.*
I think we can learn from each other.	*Ich glaube, wir können voneinander lernen.*
You scratch my back and I'll scratch yours.	*Eine Hand wäscht die andere.*

PAIR WORKS ON SMALL TALK TOPICS

In this appendix you can find suggestions for small talk situations which you can act out in pairs in the classroom. You should take 15 minutes to prepare your role using *Small Talk for Big Business* to help you.

List of situations

1. Your company is working closely together with a partner in the UK. Mr Johnson, a sales manager, is visiting your company in Germany. You have to go to lunch with him. One member of the pair is Johnson, one is the German host. Build up the appropriate small talk. (Help on page 161)

2. Your company has sold a major product to a customer in Russia. The customer arrives at Frankfurt Airport. You have to meet him and entertain him for two hours. Build up the dialogue. (Help on page 165)

3. There is a party at your new company. You should introduce yourself and small-talk your way into acceptance. Your partner has worked at the company for twenty years. (Help on page 174, 175)

4. You're sitting on the train going to England. You're in the Channel Tunnel. Build up the small talk with the nervous person sitting opposite to you. (Help on page 178, 173)

5. A person who works at your company, but who you do not know well meets you by accident at the *Weihnachtsmarkt*. Do your small talk thing! (Help on page 182)

6. You're at a brunch organised by some friends from work. You are introduced to the lady who cooked most of the things. You are left alone with her. Build up the "polite noises". (Help on page 185, 186)

7. You meet your old friend who you haven't seen for years. Unlock a few old memories from those good old days. (Help on page 183, 184)

8. You've just played tennis with a member of the club. Now you're in the bar. Build up the small talk. Find the common ground. (Help on page 185)

9. You're sitting having breakfast in a nice café. A group of students are discussing a topic which is important for you, too. Get into conversation with one of them. You have strong opinions on the topic. Take a stand! (Help on page 187, 188)

10. By accident you have to share a table with the managing director of a large local company. You might be able to offer your services there, too. How do you approach the subject ? Explore your business opportunities! (Help on page 188)

KEY TO THE EXERCISES

CHAPTER 2

Nations	Mark
British, Americans	1
Chinese, Russians	3
French, Australians, Canadians	2
Finns, Swedes, Japanese	4
Mexicans, Peruvians, Argentinians	1
Germans	4

Source: Richard D. Lewis. When Cultures collide. London 1996

CHAPTER 3

TASK 1: Spot the mistake

1. Did you have a good *journey*. (voyage: Seereise)
2. It's *good* to see you here again. (schön = gut, angenehm: good)
3. I want to begin by thanking you for *having taken* the trouble to ...

TASK 2: Guided translation

1. I beg your pardon, where is the *information desk*, please?
2. Are you here *on business*?
3. *May I ask* why you are here?
4. *Are you also staying* at the Hilton?
5. *What do you expect* from this congress?
6. Can you *recommend* me a good restaurant?
7. *Excuse me*, may *I have a look* at your program?
8. Can you tell me where the press conference *is going to take place*?

Spot the mistake

1. If you *ask* me, I would say that we should buy Irish castles.
   (*would* im Bedingungssatz nur in Ausnahmefällen)
2. I see it a little *differently*. Irish castles are too small for ...
   (hier brauchen wir das Adverb; *different* ist Adjektiv)
3. *As* I see it, German castles are more suitable for wine-growers.
   (*how* = wie ist Fragewort; hier brauchen wir die Konjunktion *as*)
4. *As far as I'm concerned*, I think we should only sell titles.
   (*concern* heißt zwar betreffen; aber: was mich betrifft: *as far as I'm concerned*)

CHAPTER 4

TASK 1: Introduction right and wrong

1A Bei der ersten Begegnung: "How do you do, Mr Brausewitz?"
2C Auf "How do you do?" reagiert man mit "How do you do?"
3B Bei der zweiten Begegnung: "How are you, Mr Dobson?"
4B "How are you?" ist eine Frage: Antwort: – "Fine, thank you."
5A "By the way, call me Paul."

TASK 2: Test your business etiquette

1C It all starts with a handshake.
2D Etiquette used to demand that the younger person, the gentleman, the subordinate wait for the older person, the lady, the superior to offer to shake hands. Today reaching out to shake hands should be almost simultaneous.
3B It is worth checking your grip: a weak one gives the impression that you are weak, too. Don't pump the others fellow's hand with an iron grip. The proper handshake is firm and dry and held for just two or three seconds.
4B Yes, I'm afraid we do.

CHAPTER 5

TASK 2: | Identifying small talk skills

1 Use a one-line joke that suits the occasion as an ice breaker.
6 Be interested in your partner's situation. Show sympathy.
2 Be considerate. An apology is a good small talk starter.
7 Use your hobbies to build bridges to your partner's interests.
3 Watch your partners. Are they in the mood to small-talk? Talk about what you're thinking at the moment.
5 Make them a gift. Find something to compliment them on.
4 Find common ground.
9 Make your name memorable.
8 Be modest. Give them the feeling that they are superior.
10 Make your job interesting. Create yourself a tag line.
11 Prepare the next encounter.

TASK 2: | Patchwork – apologies, excuses and criticism

1. *Forgive me* for saying so, but that's the way we've always done it.
2. *Excuse me*, but that's his job, not mine.
3. *Sorry*, darling, not here, somebody might see us.
4. I'm *sorry to* have to say this, ...
5. I owe you a bit of an *apology*. I've smoked your last Havana.
6. I beg your *pardon*, but this is my coat.
7. I *apologise* for being late, sir. Has anything happened?
8. I'm *afraid* we all make mistakes, don't we?

TASK 3: | Guided translation

1. I hadn't *expected* such a good interview.
2. I*'ve heard a lot about* your clever handling of complaints.
3. Your design for the new car *is really good*.
4. *What a beautiful* garden you have!
5. I'd like to *congratulate* you on your latest book.

TASK 4: Guess who I am

What's my line?

1	I'm the greatest debtor in Germany	E	Minister of Finance
2	I work for you	D	Civil Servant
3	I work in the field	F	Salesman
4	My aim is your success	A	Consultant
5	I cook the books	C	Accountant
6	I'm the polisher of the staff	B	Personnel manager

CHAPTER 6

TASK 1: Recognising small talk skills

1	Don' be a wallflower	8	Know when to talk about business
7	Build bridges	3	Interview without interrogating
5	Exchange memories		
4	Give before you take		
2	Use fade-ins		
6	Use the springboard technique		

TASK 2: Translation exercise

1	Aha! Ich verstehe.	Hmm, I see.
2	Erzählen Sie mir mehr davon.	Tell me more.
3	Kaum zu glauben!	You wouldn't believe it!
4	Ist das wirklich Ihr Ernst?	Do you really mean that?
5	Was Sie nicht sagen!	You don't say!
6	Das ist höchst interessant.	That's most interesting.
7	Hätte ich nie geglaubt.	I'd never have believed it.

TASK 3: Complete the bridges

That *reminds* me of a story I *heard* the other day.
When you mentioned Tom, I *remembered* how I first met him.
I *had* a similar experience a couple of years ago. It was in ...
Talking about holidays, what are your plans for this year?

TASK 4: Patchwork

1. If you aren't expecting anybody, do you *mind* if I join you?
2. I hope you've *recovered* from the flight. It was a bit bumpy.
3. *May I* get you anything else, a glass of wine perhaps?
4. I would be pleased if you would *honour* me with your company.
5. But *I shouldn't* be boring you with our little problems.
6. I didn't really *want* to waste your time with that now.
7. I *hope* you're settling in at your new job.
8. I didn't *want* to cause any trouble. Please let me put it right now.
9. It's really a bit chilly here. *Shall* I close the window?
10. Perhaps we *could* play a game of chess sometime.

CHAPTER 7

TASK 1: Recognising the small talk skills

2   Complimenting indirectly
1   Integrating a newcomer
5   Leap of imagination (springboard technique)
4   Reviving a conversation
3   Small talk with a purpose (two examples)

TASK 2: Guided translation

1. Hilary, have you *got a minute*?
2. John, could you *come over here for a moment*?
3. You all *seem to know each other*.
4. Is fishing *one of your many talents*, Fritz?
5. That's all true but look at it *from another point of view*.
6. I'm here *to learn more about* marketing on the Internet.
7. *I'm hoping / I hope to meet people* who have experience with computers.

CHAPTER 8

TASK 1: Are the following statements true or false?

Brausy has come to Newbury with two purposes in mind.	T
Brausy has been over-interrupting Sir Antony.	T
Sir Anthony is interested in fishing and golfing.	F
Sir Anthony thinks that Brausy is a bad small-talker.	T

TASK 2: Five small talk sins

Don't talk for too long.	5
Don't force a topic onto your partner.	4
Don't be insensitive to your partner's situation.	1
Don't ask questions that you answer yourself.	2
Don't ask for favours without having something to offer.	3
Don't unlock memories that your partner cannot share with you.	5

TASK 3: Guided Translation

1. How fascinating! That *reminds me of* ...
2. I'd like to *add something* here, if I may.
3. I *don't want* to interrupt *you*, but ...
4. Excuse me, sir, may I *ask you a question*?
5. Excuse me, but may I *play* the devil's advocate *for a moment*?

TASK 3: Patchwork: How to go on after being interrupted

1. As I was *saying* ...
2. If I could just *continue* ...
3. To *return* to my subject ...
4. *Coming* back to my story ...
5. Going back *to what* I was saying ...
6. To *go* back to what I was saying ...
7. I'll *answer* your question in a minute.
8. You *took* the words right out of my mouth.

CHAPTER 9

If a swamp alligator could talk, it would talk like Tennessee Williams.	**9**
I can write better plays than any living dancer and dance better than any living playwright	**5 / 3**
Oscar Wilde: Do you mind if I smoke? Sarah Bernhardt: I don't care if you burn.	**7**
You don't know a woman until you've met her in court.	**10**
Lewis Morris (*on being overlooked for the poet laureateship*): It is a conspiracy of silence against me – a conspiracy of silence. What should I do? Oscar Wilde: Join it.	**7**
Women are like elephants to me; they're nice to look at, but I wouldn't want to own one.	**10**
Ruth Gordon: (*explaining her latest role*) The stage is empty. There's no scenery at all. In the first scene I'm standing on the left side of the stage and the audience has to imagine that I'm eating dinner in a restaurant. Then in scene two, I'm running to the right side of the stage and the audience imagines that I'm in the drawing room. George S. Kaufmann: And the second night you have to imagine that there is an audience out front.	**1**
René B. phoned a former student who was a well-known psychiatrist "Doctor, I'm having a wonderful holiday on the Bahamas. Please tell me what is wrong."	**6**

1. Don't bore people with too many details: Lord Canterville's ghost story was too long and contained too many details.
2. Don't be a bigot in any matter or meeting: Mr Otis is the typical example of an American bigot.

TASK 3: Disagreeing politely

1. To be honest, I can't *quite* agree with you.
2. With respect, I see it *a little* differently.
3. I'm sorry, I don't *quite* agree with you. After all ...
4. I'm afraid there must be *a slight* misunderstanding.

TASK 4: Match them

1 b; 2 c; 3 a

1 I see what you mean, although ...	**b** I don't disagree altogether. Still ...
2 With due respect, what you are saying is impossible.	**c** To be quite frank, you're completely mistaken.
3 I'm afraid I can't see your point there.	**a** We'll have to agree to differ.

CHAPTER 10

TASK 1: Identifying small talk skills

He unlocks memories to meet on common ground.	2
He uses distance to signal the change in the conversation.	6
He uses body language to prepare an important proposal.	5
He wants to win a network partner.	7
He is sensitive and lets Lord Gilmore choose the topic.	3
Brausy compliments Lord Gilmore indirectly.	1
He plays the devil's advocate to provoke a decision.	4

TASK 2: Small talk etiquette

Don't misunderstand me – my dislike for you is purely platonic. *Herbert Beerbohm Tree*	T
When I want a peerage, I shall buy one like an honest man. *Lord Northcliffe*	P
One should never be unnecessarily rude to a lady except in streetcars. *O. Henry*	M
The louder he talked of his honour, the faster we counted our spoons. *R.W. Emerson*	I
I'd rather eat shit than wear a suit. *Bill Carter*	A
I much prefer travelling on British ships. There's none of that nonsense about women and children first. *Somerset Maugham*	C

TASK 3: Let's practise toasts

1. *Here's* to the beautiful bride.
2. I want to *wish* the newly wed couple all the best.
3. I rise to *toast* our Japanese guests.
4. I'd like to *make a toast* to our new colleague.
5. Let's *raise* our glasses to the *future of* Gilmore Castle.
6. I'd like to *propose* a toast to the conclusion of our contract.
7. Best of *luck,* you two. And now everybody, *bottoms* up!
8. Gentlemen, let's *celebrate* this with a glass of champagne.

CHAPTER 11

TASK 1: Recognising small talk sinners

The Missionary	3
The Schoolmaster	4
The Bigot	5
The Boaster	1
The Insensitive	2

CHAPTER 12

TASK 1: Using the Adam-Formula

Question	No.
A-bout question	2
D-rill question	1
A-id question	4
M-irror question	3

TASK 2: Spot the mistake

1. I'm so glad you introduced *me* to the world of ghosts.
2. It's been fascinating *listening to* your memories from the past.
3. It's nice to meet an eyewitness from King John's *court*.

TASK 3: More mistakes for you to spot

1. I'm going to send you that article *about* haunted castles.
2. I'll be thinking *about* your suggestions over the weekend.
3. I'll get back to you *at* the weekend to resume our conversation.

CHAPTER 13

TASK 1: Which of the deadly sins has Joe not committed?

Thou shalt not

1. bore people with too many details ✓
2. interrupt them when they talk about their problems ✓
3. boast of your own achievements
4. over-question people in a negative way
5. try to be better than another
6. try to seek free advice at the expense of another ✓
7. refuse to adapt to another's mood
8. be insensitive to your partner's problems
9. evaluate or look down on the lives of others
10. be a bigot on any matter or in any meeting

TASK 2: Say it the soft way

1. I'd like to meet a little earlier.
2. Would Friday be convenient?
3. Wouldn't that be a bit too late?
4. I might / would need a little more time.
5. I'm not very happy with that idea.

TASK 3: Test your EQ

The more points you have got, the better you are able to overcome obstacles and setbacks.

Your choice	Points	Your choice	Points
1B	1	5A	1
2A	1	6B	1
3B	1	7B	1
4B	1	8A	1

CHAPTER 14

TASK 1: Recognising small talk techniques

Noticing statement to start a conversation	2
The springboard technique	4
The psychoanalyst's technique	3
Trying to find a network partner	1

Brausy uses a springboard (leap of imagination) to change the subject because he feels that it would be painful for the lord. He avoids talking about the present situation.

TASK 2: Say it the soft way

1. I *was wondering* if you'd come to a decision yet.
2. *Wouldn't it be a better* idea to make an *earlier* decision?
3. *I'm afraid / With respect*, we need more research. *Wouldn't* we need a little *more* research before we can make a decision?
4. That's not a *very practical* decision.
5. *Honestly / With respect*, I don't really like that idea much.

CHAPTER 15

TASK 1: Identifying small talk skills

Small talk skill	No.
The psychoanalyst's technique	3
That sign of sparkle	5
Proposing a toast	1
Small talk with a purpose	
Finding common ground	2

TASK 2: Complete the speech functions

1. The reason for our *gathering* is …
2. The *occasion* of today's meeting is …
3. The *reason* for our coming together is to …
4. I'm glad to have the *chance* to speak to you about …
5. Nothing gives me greater *pleasure* …
6. I've been asked to *propose* a toast to …
7. To put it in a *nutshell*: All's well that ends well.
8. Thank you for your *attention*, ladies and gentlemen.

TASK 3: Rearrange the speech

I've been asked to propose a toast to the health of Ron and Anne. Nothing gives me greater pleasure.

Little did I think when I first saw Anne torturing the cat at the age of five that she would one day become the manager of a successful company and a loving wife.

I'm not going to say anything about Ron because he has the stature of a Sumo ringer and we all know his temper.

I've often used Sydney Smith's definition: Marriage resembles a pair of shears so joined that they cannot be separated, often moving in opposite directions, yet always punishing anyone who comes between them.

So I will conclude by raising my glass to the health of the young couple. Let's wish them all the best for a successful first marriage.

Illustration: Britta Lembke

Geschäftsbesuche, Briefe, Telefonate, Verhandlungen und Meetings verlangen ein klares sprachliches Konzept. Die Serie **Business Englisch** von **René Bosewitz** und **Robert Kleinschroth** hilft praxisnah und übersichtlich in allen Standardsituationen: mit griffigen Dialogen und informativen Texten, mit didaktisch ausgereiften Übungen und nicht zuletzt mit viel Witz.

René Bosewitz/Robert Kleinschroth
Better than the Boss
Business English fürs Büro
3-499-60138-9

René Bosewitz/Robert Kleinschroth
Better Your Business Englisch
*Crashprogramm zum Meistern
typischer Probleme*
3-499-608464-4/61448-0

René Bosewitz/Robert Kleinschroth
Check Your Language Level
Business English auf dem Prüfstand
3-499-60268-7

René Bosewitz/Robert Kleinschroth
Get Through at Meetings
*Business English für Konferenzen
und Präsentationen*
3-499-60262-8

René Bosewitz/Robert Kleinschroth
Get Through at Meetings
*Business English für Konferenzen
und Präsentationen.
Buch mit Audio-CD*
3-499-60265-2

3-499-61448-0

Illustration: Cathrin Günther

René Bosewitz/Robert Kleinschroth
Get Through at Meetings
*Business English für Konferenzen
und Präsentationen.
Buch mit Tonkassette*
3-499-60266-0

René Bosewitz/Robert Kleinschroth
How to Communicate Effectively
*Verstehen und verstanden werden
im Business*
3-499-61146-5

René Bosewitz/Robert Kleinschroth
How to Phone Effectively
Business English am Telefon.
3-499-60139-7/61449-9
Buch mit Audio-CD
3-499-60146-X/64156-1
Buch mit Tonkassette
3-499-60147-8

René Bosewitz/Robert Kleinschroth
Idioms at Work
*Bessere Geschäfte
mit treffendem Englisch*
3-499-61333-6

René Bosewitz/Robert Kleinschroth
Manage in English
Business rund um die Firma
3-499-60137-0

René Bosewitz/Robert Kleinschroth
Master Your Business Phrases
Sprachmodule für den Geschäftsalltag
3-499-60725-5

3-499-61146-X

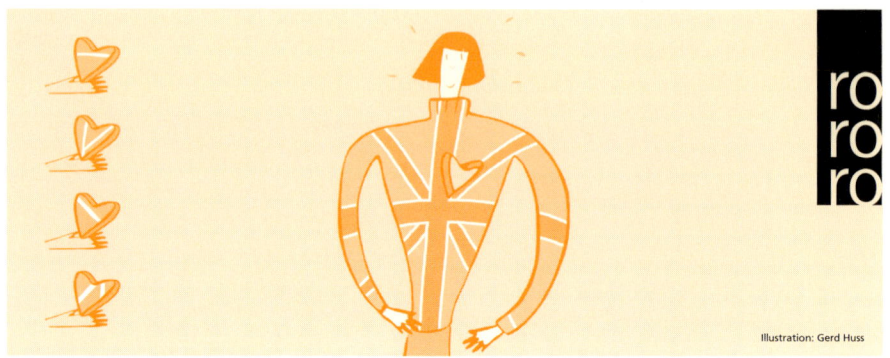

Illustration: Gerd Huss

Gunther Bischoff
Better Times
Ein leichtes Programm zum richtigen
Gebrauch der englischen Zeiten
3-499-17987-3

Gunther Bischoff
Speak you English
Programmierte Übung zum Verlernen
typisch deutscher Englischfehler
3-499-16857-X

René Bosewitz
Better Your English
Wie man typische deutsche Fehler
verlernt
3-499-60802-2

René Bosewitz
Perfect Your English
Wie man die typischsten Sprachfallen
vermeidet
3-499-61147-3

Hartmut Breitkreuz
False Friends
Stolpersteine des
deutsch-englischen Wortschatzes
3-499-18492-3

Emer O'Sullivan/DietmarRösler
Modern Talking
Englisches Quasselbuch mit Sprüchen
und Widersprüchen
3-499-18427-3

3-499-61147-3

Illustration: Gerd Huss

**Spanisch lernen: alltagsnah und von Anfang an.
Für das Lernen allein oder in der Gruppe.**

Christof Kehr/Ana Rodriguez Lebrón
Spanisch
von Anfang an
3-499-60475-2
Buch mit Audio-CD
3-499-60437-X
Buch mit Tonkassette
3-499-60476-0

Christof Kehr/Ana Rodriguez Lebrón
Spanisch 2
Der Aufbaukurs
Buch mit CD-ROM
3-499-61108-2

Christof Kehr
Spanisch in letzter Minute
Sprachkurs für Überflieger
3-499-60917-7

Christof Kehr
Spanisch in letzter Minute
Sprachkurs für Überflieger
Buch mit Audio-CD
3-499-60918-5
Buch mit Tonkassette
3-499-60919-3

3-499-60918-5